THE NEW LAW ON SECULAR INSTITUTES

A Historical Synopsis and a Commentary

THE CATHOLIC UNIVERSITY OF AMERICA
CANON LAW STUDIES
No. 347

The New Law on Secular Institutes

A HISTORICAL SYNOPSIS AND A COMMENTARY

A DISSERTATION

SUBMITTED TO THE FACULTY OF THE SCHOOL OF CANON LAW OF THE CATHOLIC UNIVERSITY OF AMERICA IN PARTIAL FULFILLMENT OF THE REQUIREMENTS FOR THE DEGREE OF DOCTOR OF CANON LAW

BY

REV. DONNELL ANTHONY WALSH, A.B., J.C.L.
PRIEST OF THE ARCHDIOCESE OF SAN FRANCISCO

THE CATHOLIC UNIVERSITY OF AMERICA PRESS
WASHINGTON, D. C.
1953

NIHIL OBSTAT:

Clemens V. Bastnagel, J.U.D.
Censor Deputatus

Washingtonii, D.C., die aprilis 1953

IMPRIMATUR:

✠ Joannes J. Mitty, D.D.
Archiepiscopi Sancti Francisci

Sancti Francisci, die maii 1953

Printed by Theo. Gaus' Sons, Inc., Brooklyn 1, N. Y., U. S. A.

IOANNI IOSEPHO MITTY D D

EMO ET RMO STI FRANCISCI ARCHIEPISCOPO

SACRA ALENDI STUDIA

STUDIOSISSIMO ATQUE LIBERALISSIMO

SCRIPTOR EX PIETATE

TABLE OF CONTENTS

PAGE

FOREWORD xi

PART I

THE EVOLUTION OF THE JURIDIC STATES OF PERFECTION

CHAPTER

I. BEFORE THE COUNCIL OF TRENT (1545-1563) 3

Article I. Preliminary Notions 3

Article II. The First Three Centuries 6

Article III. From the Fourth Century to the IV General Council of the Lateran (1215) 8

Section. 1. The individual practice of perfection.. 8

Section 2. Monasticism 10

Section 3. Canons and Canonesses 14

Section 4. The Military Orders 16

Article IV. From the IV General Council of the Lateran (1215) to the Council of Trent (1545-1563) 18

Section 1. The Mendicant Orders 20

Scholion. The Third Orders 22

Section 2. Communities without vows 23

A. Beguines and Beghards 23

B. The Brothers and Sisters of the Common Life 25

C. The Oblates of St. Frances of Rome 27

TABLE OF CONTENTS (Continued)

CHAPTER PAGE

II. From the Council of Trent (1545-1563) to the Present Day 28

Article I. The Status of Congregations of Simple Vows 28

Section 1. Religious Congregations of Women 28

Section 2. Religious Congregations of Men 33

Article II. Societies of the Common Life 36

Scholion. Proper designation of these Societies 41

III. The Rise of Secular Institutes 44

Article I. Historical Background 44

Article II. Outline of the History and Nature of the Most Prominent Secular Institutes 51

TABLE OF CONTENTS (Continued)

PART II

Legal Commentary

CHAPTER PAGE

IV. The General Concept of Secular Institutes.... 61

Article I. Definition of Secular Institutes 61
Section 1. The nature of secular Institutes....... 61
Section 2. The purpose of secular Institutes...... 62
Section 3. Divisions of secular Institutes 63

Article II. Proper Terminology 64

Article III. The Nature and Binding Force of This Constitution 67

V. The Juridic Position of Secular Institutes..... 70

Article I. Non-Religious Character of Institutes...... 70
Section 1. Absence of public vows and of the common life 70
Section 2. Exclusion of law governing religious... 74

Article II. Legislation Governing Secular Institutes 76

Article III. Competence of the Roman Congregations 79
Section 1. The Sacred Congregation of Religious 79
Section 2. The Sacred Congregation of the Council 82

VI. Essential Elements of Secular Institutes...... 84

Article I. Profession of the Evangelical Counsels.. 85

Article II. Incorporation 92

Article III. Possession of Common Houses 94

TABLE OF CONTENTS (Continued)

CHAPTER PAGE

VII. Establishment of Secular Institutes 98

Article I. Institutes of Diocesan Approval 98

Section 1. Competent authority 98

Section 2. Prescribed procedure 101

Article II. Institutes of Pontifical Approval 105

VIII. Secular Institutes in their External and Internal Relations 110

Article I. Subjection to the Local Ordinary 110

Article II. Internal Government 113

IX. Effect of this Apostolic Constitution 118

Conclusions 122

Appendix 124

Bibliography 129

Abbreviations 138

Alphabetical Index 140

Biographical Note 143

Canon Law Studies 145

FOREWORD

Scholars who are familiar with the unparalleled history of the Catholic Church sometimes set down its unyielding adherence to immutable principles as the key to its unique character. It cannot be denied that the Church throughout the centuries has maintained inviolable—often at great cost—the changeless principles on which and for which it stands. At the same time, it is no less true to state that the Church has always shown a willingness to adapt itself to the changing circumstances of particular times and places. Without the slightest compromise in essentials and without sacrificing in the least its characteristic unity, the Church has adapted itself to changing times and varying types of society.

This flexibility is clearly shown in the history of religious institutes approved by the Church. The very variety of such groups is itself proof that men and women have grouped themselves together to cope with the different problems that have arisen in the history of the Church. In the words of Pope Pius XI (1922-1939),[1]

> Although finally all [i.e. religious institutes] strive after one and the same object, yet they each have their own field of industry and labor, distinct in some way from all others. For Divine Providence so ordains that, as often as new needs must be met, new religious institutes likewise arise and flourish.

In accordance with this policy of encouraging new religious institutes to care for newly-arising needs, the Holy See has quite recently recognized an entirely new form of evangelical perfection. In the Apostolic Constitution *Provida Mater Ecclesia* of February

---

[1] Ep. ap. *Unigenitus Dei Filius,* 19 mart. 1924—*Acta Apostolicae Sedis, Commentarium Officiale* (Romae, 1909-1929; Civitate Vaticana, 1929—), XVI (1924), 133-134 (hereafter cited *AAS*); translation taken from Creusen, *Religious Men and Women in the Code* (translated by E. F. Garesché, 4 Eng. ed. by A. C. Ellis, Milwaukee: The Bruce Publishing Co., 1940), p. 287.

2, 1947, Pope Pius XII has given official approbation to societies whose members, desirous of attaining Christian perfection and of exercising a full apostolate, profess the evangelical counsels *in the world.*[2] These new societies, officially called secular Institutes, differ from religious institutes and Societies of the Common Life in that they do not impose upon their members the obligation of the common life. Rather, it is hoped that members of secular Institutes, living separately in the world and wearing secular dress, can exercise an effective apostolate in an environment closed to those known to be religious.

The first part of this dissertation is intended as a historical background to the new legislation for secular Institutes. While it will give some attention to societies of earlier centuries which in some way approximated what are now known as secular Institutes, this synopsis has for its chief aim the presentation of the juridic outlook of the Church on the various forms of the religious life as they appeared in the course of history. It will be seen that the requirements demanded by the positive law of the Church for the official recognition of states of perfection have undergone a gradual, well-defined evolution, which has reached its culmination in the approval of secular Institutes.

The second section of the present work consists of a brief commentary on the *Lex Peculiaris Institutorum Saecularium,* which appeared as an appendix to the Apostolic Constitution *Provida Mater Ecclesia.* The commentary will treat only of those matters which are included within the scope of the ten Articles of this Special Law. Special attention will be given to those portions of the law which are distinctively new; the writer considers it unnecessary to comment on those canons of the Code which have been applied without modification to secular Institutes.

Since the legislation on secular Institutes is of such very recent origin, the writer realizes that it is impossible at the present time to offer anything approaching a definitive study. However, even an introductory and compendious treatment may prove helpful to bishops and chancery officials when they are approached for permission to establish one of these Institutes. It is also hoped that

[2] *AAS,* XXXIX (1947), 114-124.

this dissertation may be of some assistance to confessors and spiritual directors in guiding souls who seem to have a vocation to live a consecrated life in the world.

The writer welcomes this occasion to acknowledge his sincere gratitude to His Excellency, the Most Reverend John J. Mitty, D.D., Archbishop of San Francisco, for the opportunity of advanced study in Canon Law at the Catholic University of America. The writer also wishes to thank the members of the Faculty of the School of Canon Law, Father Joseph E. Haley, C.S.C., M.A., Father Paul Zammit, O.P., S.T.D., Ph.D., LL.D., and all others whose scholarly guidance, helpful suggestions, and kind encouragement have made this dissertation possible

PART I

The Evolution of the Juridic States of Perfection

CHAPTER I

Before the Council of Trent (1545-1563)

Article I. Preliminary Notions

The mission of the Catholic Church, in imitation and continuation of the mission of its Divine Founder, is the sanctification and salvation of souls. During His life on earth, Christ taught by word and example what men must do to attain everlasting life. In addition to laying down the precepts which are binding upon all, Our Lord urged His followers to the pursuit of perfection through the practice of the evangelical counsels.

It is clear from the words of the New Testament itself that perfection demands something over and above what is merely required for salvation.[1] A most suitable and efficacious means of attaining the complete consecration implied in Christian perfection is to be found in the observance of the three general counsels of poverty, chastity, and obedience, by which a man devotes his possessions, his bodily faculties, and his will to the service and love of God.

From the very earliest days of the Church up to the present time, there have been legions of heroic men and women who have striven for perfection through the practice of the evangelical counsels. However, it must be stated at the very outset that this study is not intended as a history of spirituality in general; rather, it will treat of those whose practice of perfection reflects a fixed and

[1] Gospel according to St. Matthew, XIX, 16-21. Cf. St. Thomas Aquinas, *Summa Theologica* (22. ed., 6 vols., Taurini-Romae: Marietti, 1939), II IIae, q. 184, art. 3; Suarez, *De Religione,* Tr. VII, lib. 1, cap. 10, n. 3—*Opera Omnia* (26 vols. in 28, editio nova a Carolo Berton, Parisiis: apud Ludovicum Vivès, 1856-1868), XV, 49; Bouix, *Tractatus de Jure Regularium* (2 vols., Parisiis, 1857), 1, 35 (hereafter cited *De Jure Regularium*)*;* Peinador, "De Perfectione Christiana," *Commentarium pro Religiosis* (Romae, 1920-1934; ab anno 1935: *Commentarium pro Religiosis et Missionariis*), XXIX (1950), 44-60 (hereafter tihs periodical will be cited *CpR* or *CpRM*).

abiding character, and who therefore fall within the province of the legislator. In other words, this historical summary does not concern itself with the intermittent practice of private asceticism, but rather with the state of perfection and that state as recognized by the legislation of the Church.

The word "state" clearly implies the notion of stability,[2] which results from a permanent cause that cannot be changed with facility;[3] in the simple words of St. Thomas (1225-1274): "As long, then, as a man is free to abandon the works of perfection, he is not in a state of perfection."[4] This stability arises from the freely contracted obligation of striving after perfection in a special way. To be constituted in a state of perfection, it does not suffice that a person simply desire perfection; he must dedicate himself to this purpose by means of an obligation which is binding in conscience and before God. Even if a person were actually to practice perfection without having explicitly obliged himself to this pratice, he could not be said to be in a state of perfection.[5] *Ex rei natura,* therefore, the state of perfection exists whenever the profession of complete evangelical perfection is made to God, and this profession has for its means the observance of the general counsels in some fixed and abiding manner.[6]

---

[2] Cf. the definition of the religious state given in the Code of Canon Law: ". . . stabilis in communi vivendi modus. . ."—Can. 487.

[3] Canals, "Los Institutos Seculares de Perfeccion y Apostolado," *Revista Española de Derecho Canonico* (Salamanca, 1946 —), II (1947), 823-824. Cf. also Bouix, *De Jure Regularium,* I, 5-8; Wernz-Vidal, *Ius Canonicum ad Codicis Normam Exactum* (7 tomes in 8 vols., Tom. III, *De Religiosis,* Romae: apud Aedes Universitatis Gregorianae, 1933), III, 3 (hereafter cited *Ius Canonicum*).

[4] *The Religious State* (ed. John Proctor, Westminster: The Newman Press, 1950), p. 135.

[5] It may be necessary to point out that a person can be perfect without being in a state of perfection, and, conversely, a person can be in a state of perfection without actually being perfect.—*Summa Theologica,* II IIae, q. 184, art. 4.

[6] For various opinions as to whether *vows* are the only means that suffice to guarantee the stability postulated by this state, see the following: *Summa Theologica,* II IIae, q. 186, art. 6; Suarez: *De Religione,* Tr. VII, lib. 2, cap. 4, n. 5—*Opera Omnia,* XV, 128-129; Bouix, *De Jure Regu-*

The *juridic* state of perfection must necessarily include all the essential elements of the state of perfection considered in and of itself, and in addition must comprise all those elements which the Church may require as a prerequisite for its approval.[7] If the juridic state of perfection implies the recognition and approbation of the legislator, every individual and private form of perfection is immediately eliminated from its scope, because the legislator in this matter concerns himself only with the external forum.[8] To acquire the juridic character, a profession of perfection must be accompanied with some external solemnity, that is, it must be public, or at least semi-public.[9] When this character is present, the legislator can intervene in such a way that definite effects, sanctioned by law, follow. By juridical recognition, therefore, the state of perfection possesses not only the essential elements de-

---

larium, I, 44; Schaefer, *De Religiosis ad Normam Iuris Canonici* (4 ed., Romae: Typis Polyglottis Vaticanis, 1947), pp. 52-53 (hereafter cited *De Religiosis*); Coronata, *Institutiones Iuris Canonici ad Usum Utriusque Cleri et Scholarum* (5 vols., Vol. I, 2 ed., Taurini: Marietti, 1939), I, 605 (hereafter cited *Institutiones*); Molitor, *Religiosi Iuris Capita Selecta* (Ratisbonae, 1909), p. 7; Larraona, "Commentarium Codicis," *CpR,* II (1921), 170. Although the *religious state* cannot exist today without the taking of the three vows (can. 487), the Church does recognize as states of perfection Societies of the Common Life and secular Institutes, neither of which require, *de iure communi,* that their members take vows.—Pius XII, const. ap. *Provida Mater Ecclesia,* 2 febr. 1947 (*AAS,* XXXIX [1947], 117, 119, 120, 121).

[7] In the words of Creusen, "L'état juridique de perfection est la forme de vie dans laquelle la hiérarchie ecclésiastique reconnaît officiellement la présence,—à des degrés divers,—de l'état moral de perfection."—Les Instituts Séculiers," *Revue des Communautés Religieuses* (Louvain, 1925—), XX 1948), 137 (hereafter this periodical will be cited *RCR*).

[8] Cf. the explicit statement of Pius XII in *Provida Mater Ecclesia.*—*AAS,* XXXIX (1947), 117.

[9] For a complete treatment of this idea, cf. Gutiérrez, "Doctrina generalis theologica et iuridica de statu perfectionis evangelicae et comparatio inter eiusdem diversos gradus ab Ecclesa iuridice ordinatos," *De Institutis Saecularibus* (1 vol., incomplete, cura et studio *Commentarium pro Religiosis,* Romae, 1951), I, 272-277 (hereafter this article will be cited "Comparatio").

manded by its intrinsic nature, but also the added elements of positive law.

Article II. The First Three Centuries

The most ancient historical sources contain evidence that individuals of both sexes devoted themselves to the practice of perfection in the very earliest days of the Church. Whereas the *Acts of the Apostles* record that some of the Christians of Jerusalem practiced poverty,[10] it was rather the practice of chastity which characterized the pursuit of perfection in the early centuries of the Church. Practically all of the early Fathers of the Church made some mention of those men and women, known as "ascetics" (later called "confessors") and "virgins," who had dedicated themselves to Christ by lives of perfect continence.[11] Within the Christian communities, the example of the virgins and ascetics was a source of encouragement and edification. While they devoted themselves to works of penance and charity, there is no evidence that any special obligations of poverty and obedience were joined with the practice of celibacy.[12] During the first two centuries, the virgins and ascetics were outwardly indistinguishable from other Christians; they lived in the world, wore ordinary dress, and shared in the common life of Christian society. In proving that

[10] II, 44-45; IV, 32-33.

[11] Cf. St. Ignatius of Antioch, *Ad Polycarpum,* V, 2—Migne, *Patrologiae Cursus Completus Series Graeca* (161 vols. in 164, Parisiis, 1857-1866), V, 724 (hereafter cited *MPG*); St. Polycarp, *Ad Philippenses,* V, 3—*MPG,* V, 1009; Clement of Alexandria, *Stromata,* lib. III, *c.* 1—*MPG,* VIII, 1098-1104; St. Justin, *Apologia I pro christianis,* XV—*MPG,* VI, 349; Athenagoras, *Legatio pro christianis,* XXXIII—*MPG,* VI, 965; Tertullian, *Ad uxorem,* lib. I, cc. 7-8—Migne, *Patrologiae Cursus Completus Series Latina* (221 vols., Parisiis, 1844-1864), I, 1397-1400 (hereafter cited *MPL*); *De resurrectione carnis,* c. 8—*MPL,* II, 806; *De virginibus velandis,* c. 14—*MPL,* II, 908-910; Minutius Felix, *Octavius,* c. 31—MPL, III, 335-338; St. Cyprian, *Epistola XXXVI—MPL,* IV, 326-327; *Epistola LXII—MPL,* IV, 364-372.

[12] Cf. Crescentius a Cartosio, *De Virginibus in Primaeva Ecclesia Latina Earumque Juridicis Obligationibus ad Perfectionem* (Romae: Pontificia Universitas Gregoriana, 1943), pp. 47-51 (hereafter cited Crescentius a Cartosio).

they could live a life of perfection without withdrawing from the world, they were not unlike members of modern secular Institutes.

By the third century, the virgins and ascetics were treated with such respect and honor that they could be said to constitute a spiritual aristocracy within the Church. The lavish praise which individual bishops heaped upon those who bound themselves to virginity[13] was not mere rhetoric. The virgins and ascetics, being numbered among the orders (or special states) of the Church,[14] were assigned a privileged place, immediately after the clergy, at liturgical services.[15] In this special sign of ecclesiastical recognition is found the first trace of future legislation which was to define the special state of those who professed perfection.

Another example of ecclesiastical intervention in this early period is contained in the penal law of the time. In the middle of the third century, St. Cyprian (210-258) wrote that virgins found guilty of fornication were to be given a severe penance; those who persisted in their sin were to be excommunicated.[16] The application of this most severe penalty certainly implies ecclesiastical recognition of the vow of virginity.[17] Explicit legislation on this same evil is found in the Council of Elvira (300/306),[18] and the Council of Ancyra (314).[19]

---

[13] Cf., for example, Clement of Alexandria, *Qui dives salvetur,* c. 36—*MPG,* IX, 642; St. Cyprian, *De habitu virginum,* c. 3—*MPL,* IV, 445; St. Methodius, *Convivium decem virginum,* VII, 3—*MPG,* XVIII, 128, 129.

[14] St. Hippolytus, *Fragmenta in Proverbia*—*MPG,* X, 628; Origen, *In Numeros,* Hom. 2, c. 1—*MPG,* XII, 591.

[15] Tertullian, *De exhortatione castitatis,* c. XI—*MPL,* II, 926; *Constititiones Apostolorum,* lib. II, c. 57—Mansi, *Sacrorum Conciliorum Nova et Amplissima Collectio* (53 vols. in 60, Parisiis-Arnhem-Lipsiae, 1901-1927), I, 362 (hereafter cited Mansi). It is interesting to note that a trace of this has remained in the liturgy up to the present day; cf. the third exhortation in the Orations on Good Friday before the Mass of the Presanctified.

[16] *Epistola LXII*—*MPL,* IV, 364-372.

[17] Cf. Crescentius a Cartosio, pp. 33-34, 41-43.

[18] C. 13—Bruns, *Canones Apostolorum et Conciliorum Saeculorum IV-VII* (2 vols., Berolini, 1839), II, 4 (hereafter cited Bruns); Mansi, II, 8. This canon was incorporated in the *Concordia Discordantium Canonum* (*Decretum Gratiani*), c. 25, C. XXVII, q. 1.

[19] C. 19—Bruns, I, 69-70; Mansi, II, 519; c. 24, C. XXVII, q. 1.

Judged in the light of modern standards, the recognition that was given to those who professed perfection in the first three centuries certainly could not be called a *juridic* recognition in the strict sense of the term: the sources cited seem to indicate a merely liturgical or episcopal recognition. It must be recalled, however, that in this early period the Church's legal structure was still in the process of formation. The earliest canon law is expressed primarily in liturgical texts and in the references of the Fathers to the practices of the time, and proof or recogntion of *any state* in the Church at that time must be based on these sources.

Article III. From the Fourth Century to the IV General Council of the Lateran (1215)

Section 1. The individual practice of perfection

The individual pursuit of perfection, begun in Apostolic times, continued for many centuries in the Church, even after the introduction of the social form of perfection. By the middle of the fourth century the liturgical ceremony of the veiling of virgins was a common practice in the Church.[20] The reception of the veil was the definite act by which the profession of virginity was manifested, and was accompanied with a ceremony of consecration which was comparable in solemnity to the rite of ordination.[21] Moreover, so important was this ceremony considered that, at least in some places in the Latin Church, it was reserved to bishops alone.[22] By demanding a private vow as a preliminary proof of perseverance before anyone's admittance to the public ceremony of consecration,[23] the Church clearly distinguished between private and public profession. The Synod of Rome (396/398) made a distinction between unconsecrated and consecrated virgins, i.e., between those who had made a vow of virginity without the pub-

---

[20] St. Ambrose (ca. 340-397) assumed that this custom was already known.—*De virginibus*—*MPL,* XVI, 209 ff.

[21] Muzzarelli, *De Professione Religiosa a Primordiis ad Saec. XII* (Romae: Apud Piam Societatem Sancti Pauli, 1938), pp. 35-42 (hereafter cited Muzzarelli).

[22] II Council of Carthage (387/390), c. 3—Bruns, I, 118.

[23] St. Ambrose, *De virginitate,* lib. I, cap. 6—*MPL,* XVI, 276.

lic reception of the veil, and those whose private vow had become consecrated through a public ceremony.[24] The same distinction was recognized by Pope Innocent I (ca. 401-417)[25] and Pope Leo the Great (440-461).[26] The bestowal of the veil and the consecration of virgins was considered a public act performed by the bishop in the name of the Church, and as such approximated very closely the conditions required for public vows by present-day legislation.[27]

Among the particular councils of this period are found laws which imply some juridic recognition of the individual profession of virginity. The sanctions imposed by the Councils of Elvira (300/306) and Ancyra (314) for virgins who violated their vow were repeated in various forms by the Council of Valence (374),[28] the I Council of Toledo (400),[29] the III Council of Orléans (538),[30] and the General Council of Chalcedon (451).[31] Another example of special legislation is found in the laws which fixed the age at which virgins might be consecrated.[32]

It seems that the individual pursuit of perfection continued, to some extent at least, down through the middle ages. Gratian

---

[24] C. 2—Bruns, II, 275-276; Mansi, III, 1134-1135.

[25] *Epistola II,* cc. XIII, *XIV—MPL,* XX, 478-480; Jaffé, *Regesta Pontificum Romanorum ab condita Ecclesia ad annum post Christum natum MCXCVIII* (2 ed., correctam et auctam auspiciis Gulielmi Wattenbach curaverunt F. Kaltenbrunner, P. Ewald, S. Loewenfeld, 2 vols. in 1, Lipsiae, 1885-1888 [hereafter cited JK, JE, JL]), JK, n. 286; cc. 9, 10, C. XXVII, q. 1.

[26] *Epistola CLXVII,* cap. XV—*MPL,* LIV, 1208; JK, n. 544; c. 1, C. XX, q. 3.

[27] Can. 1308, §1.

[28] C. 2—Bruns, II, 112; Mansi, III, 493.

[29] C. 16—Bruns, I, 206; Mansi, III, 1001; c. 27, C. XXVII, q. 1.

[30] C. 16—Bruns, II, 197; Mansi, IX, 16; *Monumenta Germaniae Historica, Legum Sectio III, Concilia* (2 tomes, Tom. I, ed. Albertus Werminghoff, Hannoverae, 1904-1908), I, 79 (hereafter cited *MGH*).

[31] C. 16—Bruns, I, 29-30; Mansi, VII, 366.

[32] Cf. I Council of Saragossa (381), c. 8—Bruns, II, 14; Mansi, III, 635; Council of Hippo (393), c. 1—Bruns, I, 136; Mansi, III, 919; Council of Agde (506), c. 19—Bruns, II, 150; Mansi, VIII, 328; c. 13, C. XX, q. 1.

(†ca. 1157) mentioned the case of young women who assumed the religious habit in their own homes.[33] It is true that the glossator remarked that these were not to be considered religious unless they were incorporated into a community, even though they adopted the religious garb, renounced their possessions, and took a vow.[34]

However, the very fact that mention was made of them shows that the practice of private perfection was not unknown at that time. In the absence of any law, general or particular, requiring the common life for the practice of perfection, it is difficult to understand how those who practiced the evangelical counsels in an individual manner could be excluded from the state of perfection.

Taking into account what has been said about the public acceptance of vows by the Church in the ceremony of the consecration of virgins, one may feel warranted to conclude that the requisites for a juridic state were present in this form of life. If, however, the counsel of chastity alone was observed, to the exclusion of the other two general counsels, such a form of life could be called only an incomplete state of perfection.

Section 2. Monasticism

By the middle of the third century many fervent souls felt that the individual practice of perfection in the world did not afford sufficient and certain means of attaining the purpose they sought. Convinced that they could not practice complete evangelical renunciation as long as they lived with their families, and desiring to secure perfection at any cost, they fled from the world into places of solitude where they could practice contemplation without distraction or interruption. The eremitical life begun by St. Paul the Hermit (228-341) and carried on by his disciple, St. Antony (251-356), attracted many followers.[35] Almost at the same time,

[33] C. 7, C. XXVII, q. 1.

[34] "...numquam erit religiosa persona, quocumque modo vestem mutet, vel propriis renuntiet, vel votum emittat, nisi alicui religioni se det,"—*Glossa ordinaria* ad c. 7, C. XXVII, q. 1.

[35] St. Antony is said to have had more than 6000 disciples at the time of his death.—Steiger, "De Propagatione et diffusione vitae religiosae...," *Periodica de Religiosis et Missionariis* (Brugis, 1905-1919; ab anno 1920: *Periodica de Re Canonica et Morali, utilia praesertim Religiosis et*

a more developed form of monasticism was established by St. Pachomius (292-346). This Saint, called the Founder of Monasticism, composed the first monastic rule and introduced the notion of the common life. His nine monasteries for men and two for women, each under the direction of its own superior, formed a monastic congregation over which a common superior presided. While the eremitical life continued in various and sometimes unusual forms, especially in Syria, it was the cenobitical form of monasticism which spread most rapidly. In Asia Minor, and later throughout the entire Eastern world, the rule written by St. Basil the Great (ca. 330-379) exerted a great influence and has remained the basis of Eastern monasticism up to this day.

Introduction of monasticism in the West is generally attributed to St. Athanasius (295-373). As early as the year 350, St. Marcella (†410) founded a convent for women in Rome, and from Italy St. Martin of Tours (316-397) brought the monastic life to France where it soon flourished, especially in the great establishments of Lerins, Arles, and Marseilles. Through the efforts of St. Patrick (ca. 389-ca. 461), monasticism reached Ireland, and large communities were established there, both for men and women. St. Columban (ca. 542-615) brought from Ireland to France (Luxeuil), Switzerland (St. Gall), and Italy (Bobbio) his own severe rule which, according to Montalembert (1810-1870), "at one moment threatened to eclipse and replace the Benedictine institution in the Catholic world."[36]

The name which is commonly and justly associated with the propagation of Latin monasticism is that of St. Benedict (480-ca. 547), the Patriarch of the Monks of the West. While insisting on the common life and the strict observance of the three vows,[37] to which he added a vow of stability, St. Benedict moderated the

---

Missionariis, Brugis, 1920-1927; ab anno 1927; *Periodica de Re Morali, Canonica, Liturgica,* Brugis, 1927-1936, et Romae, 1937—), XIII (1924), 45 (hereafter this periodical will be cited *Periodica*).

[36] *The Monks of the West* (7 vols., authorized translation, Edinburgh and London: William Blackwood and Sons, 1861-1879), II, 387.

[37] Although the Rule of St. Benedict did not demand explicit vows of chastity and poverty, the vow of obedience to the Rule implied the profession of chastity and poverty as demanded by the Rule.

stricter elements found in Eastern rules and adapted them to the temperament and customs of the West. All his monks, clerical and lay, were to be under the rule of the abbot, and each separate house or monastery remained under the jurisdiction of the local bishop. So prudent and comprehensive was the Rule of St. Benedict that it is not difficult to understand its rapid and widespread acceptance. Eventually this Rule became almost the exclusive code of laws for all monasteries in the West,[38] and through the influence of St. Scholastica, the twin sister of St. Benedict, it was followed by practically all the communities of women religious from the sixth to the thirteenth centuries.[39]

Although following the Benedictine Rule, the monastery of Cluny (founded in 910) instituted a plan of centralization similar to that proposed by St. Pachomius. Under this plan more than two hundred monasteries grouped themselves together, each retaining its autonomy, but acknowledging at the same time some dependence on Cluny, whose Superior alone received the abbatial dignity. The Cistercians, founded by St. Robert of Molesmes (1027-1111) at Citeaux in 1098, retained this form of monastic congregation, but limited the authority of the abbot primate by granting more extensive powers to the general chapter. Among the more well-known Orders which adopted the Benedictine Rule may be mentioned the Camaldolese (founded by St. Romuald [952-1027] in 1012), the Vallambrosians (founded by St. John Gualbert [ca. 995-1073] in 1038), and, to some extent, the Carthusians (founded by St. Bruno [ca. 1032-1101] in 1084).

The first ecumenical council which passed legislation regarding religious was the Council of Chalcedon (451), which decreed the subjection of monks to the local bishop and demanded the bishop's consent for the erection of monasteries.[40] What is more pertinent

[38] Schaefer, *De Religiosis,* p. 22. The Rule of St. Benedict was made mandatory for all religious communities by several particular councils, e.g., the Council of Autun (670), c. 15—Mansi, XI, 124, and the I National Council of Germany (743), c. 7—Mansi, XII, 367.

[39] Augustine, *A Commentary on the New Code of Canon Law* (8 vols., Vol. III, 2. ed., St. Louis: B. Herder Co., 1919), III, 19.

[40] C. 4—Bruns, I, 26-27; Mansi, VII, 359; c. 10, C. XVIII, q. 2. This canon was repeated by the Councils of Agde (506), c. 27—Bruns, II, 151;

to this present study is the fact that the Council of Chalcedon, in various canons, forbade monks to engage in secular business,[41] and to enter the military service,[42] and decreed excommunication for monks who married.[43] These laws, extending the obligations of clerics to monks, implied the legislator's recognition of monasticism as a special state parallel to that of the clergy.

It would be impossible and unnecessary to cite the vast multi-Otude of ecclesiastical laws enacted during this period regarding the monastic state. It can be said with certainty, however, that the Church, in passing specific and detailed laws for the group of men who were known as monks, considered them as constituting a special state, distinct both from the clergy and from the laity. Moreover, since this special state had its own set of rights and duties, sanctioned by law and leading to certain canonical effects, one can regard it as having been a true juridic state which had for its end the acquiring of perfection.

It is interesting and illuminating to note that monks were considered by the Roman Civil Law of the period to be members of a special juridic state. The *Corpus Iuris Civilis,* especially the *Novellae,*[44] contain many regulations concerning monastic life, and it was clearly recognized that, by making profession, a monk adopted an entirely new status and lost that which he had had in common with other citizens.[45]

Mansi, VIII, 329; I Orleans (511), c. 22—Bruns, II, 165; Mansi, VIII, 355; Epaon 517/518), c. 10—Bruns, II, 168; Mansi, VIII, 560; *MGH, Legum Sectio III, Concilia,* I, 21; Lerida (524), c. 3— Bruns, II, 21; Mansi, VIII, 612-613; Barcelona (540/541), c. 10—Bruns, II, 28; Mansi, IX, 110; and the XVII Council of Toledo (694), c. 11—Mansi, XII, 105. It became civil law by incorporation into the *Corpus Iuris Civilis—Novellae,* V, 1.

[41] C. 3—Bruns, I, 26; Mansi, VII, 359.

[42] C. 7—Bruns, I, 27; Mansi, VII, 362.

[43] C. 16—Bruns, I, 29-30; Mansi, VII, 366.

[44] V; XXII, 5; LVII, 1; LXXVI: CXXIII, 33-34; CXXXI, 7; CXXXIII.

[45] For a thorough development of this notion, cf. Muzzarelli, pp. 103-114.

Section 3. Canons and Canonesses

For several centuries, monasticism was considered a lay state.[46] The essentially contemplative form of life led by monks was thought to be incompatible with the active life of priests having the care of souls. Entrance into the monastic state served primarily for personal sanctification, and seclusion from the world was demanded of those who were members of this state.[47]

It was always recognized, however, that secular priests, although living in the world, had the obligation of striving after perfection. St. Eusebius of Vercelli (ca. 283-371), recognizing the advantages of the common life, undertook to ordain only those who had already become monks.[48] St. Augustine (354-430) established a form of the common life for the clergy of his diocese without requiring actual entrance into the monastic state. Although not bound by definite rule, these Canons Regular, as they later came to be called, were considered by St. Augustine to have made a tacit profession of living in community for life.[49] This institution of St. Augustine, imitated by many other bishops, received a fresh impetus in the eighth century, when St. Chrodegang of Metz (ca. 712-766) composed a rule to govern the Canons of his diocese.[50] This rule received its final form when it was revised by the deacon Amalarius (ca. 780-850/851) in the early part of the ninth century. Approved by the Council of Aix-la-Chapelle (816), this rule was imposed on all the secular clergy of the Frankish Empire,[51] and various succeeding councils likewise demanded its adoption.[52]

---

[46] It was only from the ninth century onward that the majority of monks were clerics.—Kurtscheid, *Historia Iuris Canonici, Historia Institutorum* (Vol. I, *Ab Ecclesiae Fundatione usque ad Gratianum, Romae*: Officium Libri Catholici, 1941), I, 304.

[47] Cc. 1, 2, 4, 8, 10, C. XVI, q. 1. In later centruies, when it became the custom for monks to receive Holy Orders, it was necessary to pass legislation prohibiting them from undertaking the care of souls; cf. I General Council of the Lateran (1123), c. 17—Mansi, XXI, 285.

[48] St. Ambrose, *Sermo LVI, De natali Eusebii—MPL,* XVII, 719.

[49] *Sermo CCCLVI—MPL,* XXXIX, 1575.

[50] This rule is contained in its entirety in Mansi, XIV, 314-332.

[51] *MGH, Legum Sectio III, Concilia, II,* 312-421; Mansi, XIV, 147-246.

[52] Capitulary of Corteolona (825), c. 7—*MGH, Legum Sectio II, Capi-*

For several centuries the secular clergy lived in common without taking vows, but the possession of private property allowed by the rule of Aix-la-Chapelle gradually led to a decline in the observance of the common life.[53] When some canons began to live separately, others opposed this relaxation of discipline and took the vow of poverty.[54] These canons who continued to live in separate houses became known as canons secular, while those who took vows and lived a common life were called canons regular. This latter group gave rise to the foundation of many new Orders, some of which (e.g. the Norbertine Canons, or Premonstratensians, and the Croziers) exist to the present day.

As early as the seventh century there arose institutes for women which imitated the manner of life followed by the canons. Occupied with the recitation of the divine office, the care of the holy vestments, and the education of the young, these women were given the name of canonesses. Clearly distinguishing between *moniales* and *canonissae,* the Council of Chalon-sur-Saone (813) passed special legislation for the latter group,[55] and the Council of Aix-la-Chapelle (816) imposed a special rule upon them.[56] Much of the legislation in which canonesses received mention was aimed at the correction of abuses which had gradually crept into

---

tularia Regum Francorum (Tom. I, ed. A. Boretius, Hannoverae, 1883), I, 327 (Corteolona is situated in northern Italy, near Pavia); II Council of Aix-la-Chapelle (836), Cap. II, n. 15—*MGH, Legum Sectio III, Concilia, II,* 713-714, and Mansi, XIV, 683; Council of Meaux (845), c. LIII—*MGH, Legum Sectio II, Capitularia Regum Francorum* (Tom. II, edd. A. Boretius and V. Krause, Hannoverae, 1890-1897), II, 411, and Mansi, XIV, 831; Council of Rome (853), c. 7—Mansi, XIV, 1003.

[53] Cf. Stanton, *De Societatibus sive Virorum sive Mulierum in Communi Viventium sine Votis* (2. ed., Halifaxiae: Apud custodiam librariam maioris seminarii a Sanctissimo Corde B.M.V., 1936), pp. 6-7 (hereafter cited *De Societatibus*).

[54] Cf. Council of Rome (1059), c. 4—Mansi, XIX, 908; Council of Rome (1063), c. 4—Mansi, XIX, 1025.

[55] Cc. 53-65—*MGH, Legum Sectio III, Concilia,* II, 284-285.

[56] *Regula Sanctimonialium—MGH, Legum Sectio III, Concilia,* II, 421-456.

this novel form of the religious life.[57] Although the canonesses, unlike other groups of women religious, took no vows and made no form of public profession, they were explicitly recognized by Popes Boniface VIII (1294-1303)[58] and Clement V (1305-1314).[59] The institution of secular canonesses may be regarded as a legal forerunner of those communities which are today called Societies of the Common Life.[60]

Section 4. The Military Orders

In the eleventh century, the military successes of the followers of Mohammed presented a real danger to the Church. After overrunning the greater part of the Byzantine Empire, the conquerors took possession of Egypt and a portion of Spain, and finally captured Jerusalem in 1071. Aroused by the cruelties inflicted upon pilgrims, Pope Urban II (1088-1099) issued a plea to all Christendom to join in a Crusade to liberate the Holy Land. One of the effects of the Crusades was the establishment of the Military Orders, which marks a new era in the history of the religious state.

The Hospitallers of St. John of Jerusalem, later known as the Knights of Malta, were originally founded for the practice of works of mercy towards pilgrims and the sick. Shortly after adopting a rule requiring the three solemn vows (1118), they assumed a military character and took up arms in the defense of the Faith.[61]

---

[57] Cf. Council of London (1138), c. 15—Mansi, XXI, 513; II General Council of the Lateran (1139), cc. 26, 27—Mansi, XXI, 532-533; Council of Rheims (1148), c. 4—Mansi, XXI, 714-715.

[58] C. 43, *de electione et electi potestate,* I, 6, in VI°.

[59] C. 2, *de statu monachorum vel canonicorum regularium,* III, 10, in Clem.

[60] Ristuccia, *Quasi-Religious Societies,* The Catholic University of America Canon Law Studies, n. 261 (Washington, D. C.: The Catholic University of America Press, 1949), p. 6.

[61] Currier, *History of Religious Orders* (New York, 1894), pp. 10-11; 202-208.

Their rule was approved by Callistus II (1119-1124) in 1119[62] and confirmed by later pontiffs.[63]

Among other similar Military Orders may be mentioned the Teutonic Knights (1190) and the ill-fated Knights Templar (1118). A surprising innovation was the relaxation of the vow of chastity, by which members of some Military Orders were allowed to marry. Thus the Order of Calatrava[64] and the Order of St. James[65] required the vow of conjugal chastity together with the usual vows of poverty and obedience.

For the sake of convenience, various charitable Orders which came into existence at that time may be grouped with the Military Orders. The Trinitarians, founded by St. John of Malta (1160-1213) and St. Felix of Valois (1127-1212) for the redemption of Christians held captive by the infidels, were approved by Innocent III (1198-1216) in 1198.[66] With a similar purpose in mind, St. Peter Nolasco (ca. 1182-1258), with the aid of St. Ray-

---

[62] Ep. *Ad hoc nos disponente,* 2 iun. 1119—JL, n. 6700; although mentioned in *MPL,* CLXIII, 1102, the actual text is not given. Most authors, probably following the statement in the classical work of Helyot, *Histoire des ordres monastiques, religieux et militaires, et des congrégations séculières* (8 vols., Paris, 1714-1719), III, 75, give the year of approval as 1120, but a study of the sources fails to reveal any document to support this date.

[63] Anastasius IV (1153-1154), ep. *Christianae fidei,* 21 oct. 1154—*Bullarium Diplomatum et Privilegiorum Sanctorum Romanorum Pontificum Taurinensis Editio* (24 vols. et appendix, Augustae Taurinorum, 1857-1872), II, 618-621 (hereafter cited *Bull. Rom. Taur.*); JL, n. 9930, and Alexander III (1159-1181), ep. *Omne datum optimum,* ca. 1181—*Bull. Rom. Taur.,* II, 829-832.

[64] Approved by Alexander III, ep. *Justis petentium desideriis,* 25 sept. 1164—*MPL,* CC, 310-312; JL, n. 11064.

[65] Approved by Alexander III, ep. *Benedictus Deus in,* 5 iul. 1175—*Bull. Rom. Taur.,* II, 781-785; JL, n. 12504.

[66] Ep. *Operante Divinae dispositionis,* 17 dec. 1198— *Bull. Rom. Taur.,* III, 133-137; Potthast, *Regesta Pontificum Romanorum inde ab anno post Christum natum MCXCVIII ad annum MCCCIV* (2 vols., Berolini, 1874-1875), n. 483 (hereafter cited Potthast). Cf. also ep. *Operante Patre luminum,* 18 iun. 1209—*Bull. Rom. Taur.,* III, 234-236; Potthast, n. 3744, and Clement IV (1265-1268), ep. *In ordine vestro,* 7 dec. 1267—*Bull. Rom. Taur.,* III, 786-792; Potthast, n. 20180.

mond of Pennafort (1175-1275), established the Mercedarian Order, which secured papal approval in 1235.[67] Although the purpose and activities of these institutes differed completely from those of the Military Orders, the two held a similar place in history as pioneers in the uniting of the active life with the observance of the evangelical counsels.

In terms of this present study, the establishment of the Military Orders had a twofold significance. In the first place, recognition of this type of life demonstrated the Church's willingness to approve new forms demanded by changing conditions. Despite its traditional caution and fear of innovation, the Church was not slow to approve unprecedented institutes to cope with the new problems and dangers of the times. Secondly, a definite milestone in the evolution of the juridic states of perfection was to be noted in the emergence of groups pursuing perfection while engaged in the active life. Hitherto, perfection had implied a life of solitude, prayer, and contemplation. Although the canons regular had attempted to unite the ideals of perfection with the active life of the ministry, the terms "religious" and "monk" still remained almost synonymous in the popular mind. By approving the Military Orders, the Church prepared the way for the Orders of Mendicants and Clerks Regular, which were to be so successful in uniting the active with the contemplative life.

Article IV. From the IV General Council of the Lateran (1215) to the Council of Trent (1545-1563)

Before giving an account of the rise of new forms of the religious life, one must necessarily consider several important laws which were enacted during this period. In an effort to prevent the needless and dangerous multiplication of new religious societies, the IV General Council of the Lateran (1215) strictly prohibited the foundation of new religious institutes and ordered those wishing to enter a religious institute to choose one of the already

---

[67] Gregory IX (1227-1241), ep. *Devotionis vestrae precibus,* 17 ian. 1235—*Bull. Rom. Taur.*, III, 485; Potthast, n. 9825.

existing approved orders.[68] Although the wording of this canon[69] might seem to forbid completely the foundation of all new religious institutes, its effect was rather to withdraw the right of approval from the local bishops and to decree implicitly the necessity of papal approbation for the juridical recognition of a new institute.[70] This interpretation of the Lateran decree is confirmed in the II General Council of Lyons (1274). In explicitly reserving to the Holy See the prerogative of granting approval, this latter Council suppressed all institutes founded since the IV General Council of the Lateran, except those which had obtained papal opproval.[71] Moreover, as a result of this law, the individual and private practice of perfection no longer sufficed; thenceforth a person's incorporation into an approved institute was required if his status was to obtain the juridical recognition of the Church.[72]

Legislation enacted by Boniface VIII (1294-1303) had similarly far-reaching effects on the later development of the juridical states of perfection. This pontiff decreed that vows taken in a community approved by the Holy See were solemn vows [73] and required the strict observance of the cloister for all women who

---

[68] C. 13—Mansi, XXII, 1002.

[69] "Ne nimia religionum diversitas gravem in Ecclesia Dei confusionem inducat, firmiter prohibemus, ne quis de cetero novam religionem inveniat; sed quicumque voluerit ad religionem converti, unam de approbatis assumat. . ."—*Loc. cit.*

[70] This is the interpretation given by Hostiensis (Henricus de Segusio), *Commentaria in Quinque Decretalium Libros* (5 vols. in 3, Venetiis, 1581) in his commentary on the Decretal which repeats the Lateran decree, c. 9, X, *de religiosis domibus, ut episcopo sint subiectae,* III, 36, s.v. *approbatis.*

[71] C. 23—Mansi, XXIV, 96; c. un., *de religiosis domibus,* III, 17 in VI°; c. un., *de religiosis domibus,* tit. VII, in Extravag. Ioan. XXII.

[72] Cf. McFarland, *Religious Vocation—Its Juridic Concept* (Typewritten Licentiate Dissertation: The Catholic University of America, Washington, D. C., 1950), pp. 48-49; Bouix, *De Jure Regularium,* I, 207-208; Bachofen, *Compendium Juris Regularium* (Neo Eboraci, 1903), pp. 23-24.

[73] C. un., *de voto et voti redemptione,* III, 15, in VI°. If to be a religious one needed to enter an institute approved by the Holy See, and if vows taken in approved institutes were solemn vows, it follows that only those who had professed solemn vows were to be considered religious in the strict juridical sense.

made religious profession.[74] This latter decree, which eliminated the possibility of any contact with the world on the part of women religious, was binding for many centuries, and it was only in very recent times that the Church has accorded the strict title of religious to women who are not bound by the complete observance of the cloister.

Section 1. The Mendicant Orders

Despite the effect of the Gregorian reform, the state of the Church in the twelfth century was far from ideal. Lax and even scandalous conduct on the part of the clergy and the hierarchy was necessarily reflected in the life of the laity. Even in the midst of this decline of morality, however, there were many indications of the laity's desire to lead a better life. Lacking the leadership and inspiration of the clergy, lay men and women in different countries took the initiative in attempting to reestablish the ideals of perfection taught in the Gospel. These lay-inspired movements often assumed an anti-clerical character; some of them even began to propagate heresy. Such groups as the *Humiliati*, the Waldensians, and the Albigensians succeeded in winning over numerous followers who, sincere in their desire for higher moral standards, were not sufficiently instructed to realize the dangerous and erroneous tendencies of the pseudo-reform. The specious appeal of these movements presented a real danger to the faith—a danger which was providentially overcome through the etsablishment of the Mendicant Orders.

Divesting themselves of all earthly things and practicing the detachment of apostolic times, the sons of St. Francis of Assisi (1182-1226) and St. Dominic (1170-1221) earned for themselves the right to be heard when they denounced the vices of the age, and the success of their work was immediate and universal.

St. Dominic, adopting the Rule of St. Augustine,[75] received approval for his Order from Honorius III (1216-1227) on Decem-

---

[74] Const. *Periculoso—c.* un., *de statu regularium,* III, 16, in VI°.

[75] This Rule had been implicitly approved by the II General Council of the Lateran (1139), c. 26—Mansi, XXI, 532-533.

ber 22, 1216.[76] Although St. Francis sought approval for his Order in 1209 (i.e. before the IV Lateran Council), Innocent III, prudently suspicious of such new movements, granted only oral approval. Actually, formal approval was given only subsequent to the general law that forbade the foundation of new institutes which did not follow an approved rule.[77] The establishment of Second Orders for women, and the foundation of the Carmelites and Servites continued and extended the work of the original Mendicant Orders founded by St. Francis and St. Dominic.

The significance of the appearance of the Mendicant Orders lies in the official recognition of a way of life that was essentially both active and contemplative.[78] Although the monks had been responsible for a very extensive apostolic activity, this type of work had been done by way of exception from their essentially contemplative way of life; the Mendicants, on the other hand, deliberately set out to mingle with the world, without at the same time abandoning any of the observances necessary for the pursuit of perfection. A definite innovation was marked by the recognition of religious institutes which considered the work of the apostolate no less important than the work of personal sanctification.[79] By demonstrating that the strict observance of the evangelical counsels was possible without complete and perpetual seclusion from the world, the Mendicant Orders initiated a new era in the evolution of recognized states of perfection.

---

[76] Bulla, *Religiosam vitam—Bull. Rom. Taur.*, III, 309-311; Potthast, nn. 5402, 5403.

[77] Honorius III, const. *Solet annuere,* 29 nov. 1223—*Bull. Rom. Taur.*, III, 394-397; Potthast, n. 7108.

[78] Cf. the well-known phrase of St. Thomas Aquinas in which he describes the work of the Dominicans as *"contemplata aliis tradere."*

[79] E.g., the Dominican Constitution explicitly requires the superior to dispense from any detail of the monastic observance when the good of the apostolate calls for it; cf. *Constitutiones Fratrum Praedictorum,* Prologus, III—*Codex Regularium Monasticarum et Canonicarum* (6 vols., ed. L. Holstenius; ed. altera cura M. Brockie, Augustae Vindelicorum, 1759), IV, 12-13, and the commentary therein given s.v. *cum ordo noster.*

Scholion. The Third Orders

So great was the fire of enthusiasm kindled by the preaching of St. Francis that entire villages desired to abandon all things for God, husbands willing to leave their wives, and wives their husbands. The Seraphic Father prudently persuaded them to remain in their homes and serve God faithfully, at the same time promising to draw up for them a way of life which, though adapted to their secular state, would nevertheless render them in some degree similar to religious.[80] It was in this way that the Third Order of St. Francis originated.[81]

The rule drawn up for the Order of Penitence, as it was originally called, prescribed a way of life by which persons could strive after perfection while living in the midst of the world. It was not, however, a religious rule; there was no mention of the cloister for women members, nor was the taking of solemn vows required. Various privileges granted by the Holy See to Franciscan Tertiaries reflected implicit recognition, and their rule received explicit approval from Nicholas IV (1288-1292) in 1289.[82] The Dominicans, Carmelites, Servites, and other Orders likewise instituted affiliated groups for persons seeking perfection in the world.

Even in the thirteenth century, however, there began a tendency among Tertiary Orders to unite into communities. Although at first these communities did not take any religious vows, they

---

[80] Currier, *History of Religious Orders,* p. 253.

[81] It should be mentioned that this was not an entirely new concept. The Secular Oblates of St. Benedict and, to some extent, the lay auxiliaries of the Premonstratensians anticipated the idea of the laity's being affiliated, both in a material and in a spiritual manner, with religious life and institutes. A complete account of the Oblates is given in an anonymous article, "Les Oblats de St. Benoît," *Revue Bénédictine* (Bruges, 1884—), III (1886-1887), 55-61, 107-111, 156-160, 209-220, 249-255; the Premonstratensian movement is summarized in Reinmann, *The Third Order of St. Francis,* The Catholic University of America Canon Law Studies, n. 50 (Washington, D. C.: The Catholic University of America, 1928), pp. 14-16.

[82] Bulla *Supra montem—Bull. Rom. Taur.,* IV, 90-99.

more and more withdrew themselves from the world, so that before very long they added to their rules the obligations of solemn vows and of the observance of the cloister.[83]

Section 2. Communities without Vows

A. Beguines and Beghards

During this period, several attempts were made to establish communities of men and women who, though not professing any public vows, imitated the life of religious. The group of women who came to be called Beguines were founded in Holland at the end of the twelfth century.[84] The form of life they lived appealed to many widows and unmarried women who wished to devote themselves to prayer and good works without completely leaving the world. Since there was no common rule and each house was autonomous, it is difficult to describe the life of the Beguines in general terms. Ordinarily, however, the members were required to make a novitiate of two years in the central house, but after six years of community life were allowed to return to the world and live in their own homes. Instead of the usual public profession, the Beguines took only private vows which were not perpetual, but were binding only as long as they remained in the community.[85]

Similar communities for men arose in the beginning of the thirteenth century. Known as Beghards, members of these institutes were laymen who dedicated themselves to the care of the sick and to other corporal works of mercy. Without taking any public vows, they lived a life of poverty. Generally they were not obliged to

---

[83] Ristuccia, *Quasi-Religious Societies,* p. 10.

[84] Historians do not agree in recounting the origin of this institute; probably the founder was Lambert the Stammerer (*Le Bègue*), a priest of the city of Liège who died in 1177.— Helyot, *Histoire des Ordres,* VIII, 1-4; Heimbucher, *Die Orden und Kongregationen der katholischen Kirche* (3. ed., 2 vols., Paderborn: Ferdinand Schöningh, 1933-1934), II, 638. Cf. also the references cited in Stanton, *De Societatibus,* p. 18, note 56.

[85] Stanton, *De Societatibus,* pp. 19-20.

live in community, and some of them became itinerant preachers. After the foundation of the Third Order Secular of St. Francis, many of the Beghards and Beguines adopted the Tertiary Rule.

The lack of adequate ecclesiastical supervision over these communities seems to have been the cause of the laxities and errors into which their members fell. Before very long, it became necessary to pass legislation curbing these dangerous tendencies. As early as 1227, the Council of Trier forbade the Beghards to preach.[86] Both Beguines and Beghards were reproved by the Synod of Fritzlar (1259),[87] and the Provincial Council of Mainz (1261) condemned various abuses connected with their way of life.[88] Explicit condemnation of both groups was incorporated in the particular councils of Eichstätt (1282),[89] Béziers (1299),[90] and Cologne 1306).[91] Finally, the General Council of Vienne (1311-1312) enumerated and condemned the doctrinal errors held and taught by what it called "the abominable sect of wicked men, commonly called Beghards, and of faithless women, known as Beguines".[92] The same Council completely suppressed the institution of the Beguines; the penalty of excommunication was thenceforth incurred *ipso facto* by those who continued this form of life or who returned to it in the future.[93]

Pope John XXII (1316-1334) later mitigated the extreme severity of this decree so as to exempt from its provisions those members who had remained orthodox.[94]

---

[86] C. 8—Mansi, XXIII, 32.

[87] C. 4—Mansi, XXIII, 998.

[88] Cc. 23 and 45—Mansi, XXIII, 1089 and 1096.

[89] C. 26—Hefele-Leclercq, *Histoire des Conciles* (11 vols. in 21, Paris: Letouzey et Ané, 1907-1952), VI, 290-291 (hereafter cited Hefele-Leclercq). The acts of this Council are not contained in Mansi.

[90] C. 4—Mansi, XXIV, 1216-1217.

[91] In the first synod of that year held by Archbishop Henry de Virneburg (1244-1332) on February 21, 1306.—Hefele-Leclercq, VI, 599.

[92] C. 6—Hefele-Leclercq, VI, 682-684. The translation herein employed is that of Schroeder, *Disciplinary Decrees of the General Councils* (St. Louis: B. Herder Book Co., 1937), p. 389.

[93] C. 5—Hefele-Leclercq, VI, 681; c. 1, *de religiosis domibus, ut episcopo sint subiectae,* III, 11, in Clem. Cf. also c. 3, *de haereticis,* V, 3, in Clem., and c. un., *de religiosis domibus,* tit. VII, in Extravag. Ioan. XXII.

[94] C. un., *de religiosis domibus,* III, 9, in Extravag. com., summarium.

B. The Brothers and Sisters of the Common Life

Not long after the Beguines and Beghards began to prove a troublesome and dangerous element in the Church, there arose two societies which were influential in propagating the true and orthodox notion of perfection. The foundation of the Sisters of the Common Life took place at Deventer, Holland, in 1379, under the guidance of Gerard de Groote (1340-1384). Being a group of pious women who wished to live the higher life of perfection without relinquishing their lay status, these Sisters did not profess any vows nor did they wear any distinctive habit.[95] They were obliged to support themselves and were explicitly forbidden to beg. Their form of life attracted many followers, so that by the middle of the fifteenth century they had ninety separate houses,[96] but, with the passage of time, many of their number adopted either the rule of the Third Order of St. Francis or that of the canonesses of St. Augustine.

The Brothers of the Common Life were originally a group of young men whom Gerard de Groote banded together for the task of transcribing books and for the work of teaching. As their numbers grew, the mutual help and encouragement of life in common seemed desirable, and their founder was prevailed upon to allow this form of life.[97] Having priests, clerics, and laymen among their members, the Brothers did not take any vows, but they pledged themselves to remain for life in their house and to obey their superior. Each Brother was to earn the necessities of life by his own labor, and promised to give his earnings to the common fund. Even when houses were multiplied throughout Holland and Germany, a minimum of organization was retained, and each house remained completely autonomous. In presenting to the world an example of evangelical perfection, the Brothers exerted considerable influence on the religious life of the times, and their houses became known as centers in the revival of Christ-

[95] Stanton, *De Societatibus*, p. 24.

[96] Heimbucher, *Die Orden und Kongregationen der katholischen Kirche*, II, 559.

[97] Kettlewell, *Thomas à Kempis and the Brothers of the Common Life* (2. ed., abridged, London, 1885), pp. 72-73, 77-79.

ian life and spirituality. Even in our own day, one of their members, Thomas à Kempis (1380-1471), is among the most widely read of spiritual writers.

It should be noted that the Brothers did not consider their congregation to be a new religious Order, and clearly stated that they took no vows and wore no habit. When they received the approval of the Bishop of Utrecht (April 30, 1401), it was explicitly mentioned that approval was granted only on condition that a new Order had not been founded in contravention of the papal prohibition.[98] The original foundation of the Brothers of the Common Life was overshadowed by the establishment of the monastery of Windesheim, where, in compliance with the wishes of their founder, many of the Brothers took vows as Canons Regular of St. Augustine.

Gerard de Groote proved to be prophetic in warning that his followers would incur the opposition of the Mendicant Orders. The controversy that ensued has importance in that it throws some light on the theological and juridic opinion of the time regarding the practice of perfection in the world. One of the bitterest opponents of the Brothers of the Common Life, the Dominican Matthew Grabow, sought their condemnation at the Council of Constance (1414-1418). In summarizing his opinions, he proposed a number of propositions, of which the following are relevant: that it is impossible to fulfill the three evangelical counsels outside of the strict religious state, that it is gravely sinful for priests and clerics to live a common life except in approved religious Orders, and that those who live the common life outside of religious Orders sin gravely and are excommunicated.[99] In refutation of these opinions, Peter D'Ailly (1350-1420) and John Gerson (1364-1429) pointed to the example of the early Christians at Jerusalem and declared that it was false to state that the counsels could not be observed outside the religious state or with-

[98] Rothoff, *Le Droit des Sociétés sans Voeux* (Bruges: Desclée de Brouwer, 1949), p. 43, note 1.

[99] Von der Hardt, *Magnum et Oecumenicum Constantiense Concilium* (6 vols. in 3, Francofurti et Lipsiae, 1697-1700, III, 106-113; Mansi. XXVIII, 386-390.

out the taking of vows. They condemned the propositions of Grabow as erroneous, rash, and conducive to scandal,[100] and on April 3, 1418, the Council accepted Grabow's retraction of his views.[101]

C. The Oblates of St. Frances of Rome

For the sake of completeness, some mention should be made of the community established by St. Frances of Rome (1384-1440). Assembling several oblates of St. Benedict in a house called the *Torre de' Specchi* on the Capitoline Hill, St. Frances placed them under a modified version of the Benedictine Rule. No vows were to be taken, but the members were required to promise stability and obedience. Even after the completion of the novitiate, the Oblates were free to leave the community to contract marriage.[102] Not being bound by the observance of the cloister, they could obtain permission to withdraw from community life and remain in their own homes for an indefinite period.[103]

Upon the death of her husband, St. Frances herself entered this community in 1436 and was superioress until her death in 1440. The Oblates were approved by Eugene IV (1431-1447) on July 4, 1433, and seven years later the same pontiff granted them the right to share in the favors, privileges and pious acts of the religious Orders.[104]

---

[100] Von der Hardt, *op. cit.,* 112-119; Mansi, XXVIII, 390-394.

[101] Von der Hardt, *op. cit.,* IV, 1544; Mansi, XXVIII, 394; Bail, *Summa Conciliorum Omnium* (rev. ed., 2 vols., Patavii, 1723), I, 486-487.

[102] Helyot, *Histoire des Ordres,* VI, 215.

[103] Stanton, *De Societatibus,* p. 29.

[104] Baronius, *Annales Ecclesiastici* (ed. A. Theiner, 37 vols., Vols. I-XXVIII, Barri-Ducis, 1864-1875; Vols. XXIX-XXXVII, Parisiis. 1876-1883), XXVIII, 157-158.

CHAPTER II

From the Council of Trent (1545-1563) to the Present Day

Article I. The Status of Congregations of Simple Vows

Section 1. Religious Congregations of Women

After the Council of Trent had restated the Constitution *Periculoso* of Boniface VIII,[1] St. Pius V (1566-1572) required that all communities of women observe the cloister, even though their constitutions did not demand it, and despite any custom to the contrary.[2] Tertiaries living in common were commanded to take solemn vows and to assume the obligations of the cloister.[3] All communities of women in which solemn vows were not taken and the papal cloister not observed were interdicted and perpetually forbidden in the future. Such communities were condemned to a slow death, for thenceforth their receptions and professions would be invalid. The sweeping provisions of this Constitution were definite and unequivocal;[4] only after several hundred years did the

[1] Conc. Trident., Sess. XXV, *de regularibus*, c. 5.

[2] Const. *Circa pastoralis,* 29 maii 1566—*Bull. Rom. Taur.,* VII, 447-452; *Codicis Iuris Canonici Fontes,* cura Emi Petri Gasparri editi (9 vols., Romae [postea Civitate Vaticana]: Typis Polyglottis Vaticanis, 1923-1939; Vols. VII-IX ed. cura et studio Emi Iustiniani Serédi), n. 112 (hereafter cited *Fontes*).

[3] Members of Third Orders Secular who lived in their own homes were not affected by this Constitution—Bouix, *De Jure Regularium,* I, 316-317.

[4] Subsequent legislation attempted to enforce exact compliance with this Constitution: Gregorius XIII (1572-1585), const. *Deo sacris,* 30 dec. 1572—*Bull. Rom. Taur.,* VIII, 28-32, and *Fontes,* n. 143; Sixtus V (1585-1590), const. *Cum sicuti, 20 dec.* 1589—*Bull. Rom. Taur.,* IX, 138-140; S. C. Ep. et Reg., *Lisbonen,* 22 ian. 1596—*Fontes,* n. 1547; Urbanus VIII (1623-1644), const. *Pastoralis Romani Pontificis,* 13 ian. 1630, cited by Benedict XIV (1740-1758) in const. *Quamvis iusto,* 30 apr. 1749 (§ 2, VI)—*Fontes,* n. 398.

Holy See recede from this strict policy towards Congregations of women religious in simple vows.

In spite of this unmistakably clear legislation, some of the old Congregations remained in existence, and many new ones sprang up. Some indications of a more benign attitude on the part of the Holy See may be found in the latter seventeenth and early eighteenth centuries. Clement IX (1667-1669) granted certain favors to a group of women who lived in common without solemn vows;[5] later, Benedict XIII (1724-1730) indicated his unwillingness to suppress those communities of tertiaries who took only simple vows, and expressly stated that they should not be compelled either to take solemn vows or to observe the cloister.[6] Within a few years, however, Clement XII (1730-1740) revoked all the concessions and privileges granted by his predecessors in favor of women religious with simple vows,[7] and thus the provisions of the Constitution *Circa pastoralis* were restored in full force.

It remained for Clement's successor, Benedict XIV (1740-1758) to give some juridic recognition to these groups. Eminent canonist that he was, this pontiff recognized the anomalous position of those communities of women whose usefulness and fruitful work were acknowledged by all, but who were at the same time denied official approbation. In his celebrated Constitution *Quamvis iusto*[8] he gave the first juridical description of present-day institutes of women as 1) professed with simple vows; 2) not held to the observance of the cloister; 3) organized in a hierarchical order, and 4) having for their purpose the exercise of works of charity.[9] Although directed to one particular institute (The English Ladies"), this Constitution served as a basis of all subsequent legal decisions for similar institutes up to the beginning of the twentieth century.

---

[5] Const. *Alias propositas,* 10 dec. 1667—*Bull. Rom. Taur.,* XVII, 609-610.

[6] Bulla *Pretiosus,* 25 maii 1727—*Bull. Rom. Taur.,* XXII, 522-554 (cf. especially p. 542).

[7] Const. *Romanus Pontifex,* 31 mart. 1732—*Bull. Rom. Taur.,* XXIII 323-327.

[8] 30 apr. 1749—*Fontes,* n. 398.

[9] Larraona, "Commentarium Codicis," *CpR,* I (1920), 49

Without going into the background of this law,[10] one may here state that the Constitution *Quamvis iusto* granted some juridic status to Congregations of simple vows and placed them under the jurisdiction of the local ordinary.[11] The pontiff expressly stated that he did not intend to abrogate the provisions of the Constitution *Circa pastoralis,* but rather derogated from the law to the extent of giving passive toleration to the Institute in question.[12] Despite the toleration accorded them, the English Ladies were not to be considered as true religious in the canonical sense, and their vows were recognized as only simple.[13] This document,

---

[10] A summary of the occasion and text of the *Quamvis iusto* can be found in Farrell, *The Rights and Duties of the Local Ordinary Regarding Congregations of Women Religious of Pontifical Approval,* The Catholic University of America Canon Law Studies, n. 128 (Washington, D. C.: The Catholic University of America Press, 1941), pp. 26-29, and Orth, *The Approbation of Religious Institutes,* The Catholic University of America Canon Law Studies, n. 71 (Washington, D. C.: The Catholic University of America, 1931), pp. 54-57.

[11] An indirect effect of the *Quamvis iusto* was the implicit recognition of the bishop's right to establish Congregations of simple vows. The legal basis upon which bishops acted in approving new institutes, despite the prohibitions of the IV General Council of the Lateran (1215) and the II General Council of Lyons (1274), has been explained in various ways by canonists; cf. Wernz, *Ius Decretalium ad Usum Praelectionum in Scholis Textus Iuris Canonici* (6 vols., Romae, 1898-1914), III n. 610; Suarez, *De Religione,* Tr. VII, lib. 2, c. 16, n. 18—*Opera Omnia,* XV, 202-203; *Collectanea in Usum Secretariae Sacrae Congregationis Episcoporum et Regularium* (2. ed., cura A. Bizzarri Archiepiscopi Philippensis Secretarii edita, Romae: Ex Typographia Polyglotta S. C. de Prop. Fide, 1885), p. 742, note 1 (hereafter cited *Collectanea*); Chelodi, *Ius Canonicum de Personis* (3. ed. curavit Pius Ciprotti, Vicenza: Società Anonima Tipografica, 1942), p. 389, note 2; Pejška, *Jus Canonicum Religiosorum* (3. ed., Friburgi Brisgoviae: Herder, 1927), p. 13; Bouix, *De Jure Regularium,* I, 201-216; Larraona, "Commentarium Codicis," *CpR,* I (1920), 47-48; Orth, *The Approbation of Religious Institutes,* pp. 58-62.

[12] N. 23 (of *Quamvis iusto*).

[13] "...Virgines Anglicanas non esse vere Religiosas; promissiones, quae ab ipsis emittuntur, non esse ad summum, nisi Vota simplicia...", n. 13. The words *"vota simplicia"* seem to refer to what modern canonical terminology would designate as *"vota privata"*—Stanton, *De Societatibus,* p. 15.

which granted toleration to Congregations of women without recognizing them as religious, became the established guide and norm for all such Congregations until the time of the Constitution *Conditae a Christo,* which was issued by Leo XIII (1878-1903) on December 8, 1900.[14]

The political and social turmoil brought on by the French Revolution induced the Church to adopt a more favorable attitude towards Congregations of simple vows. When the monasteries lost legal recognition of their moral personality and consequently their ability to own property, and when the civil law of France recognized only simple (and temporary) religious vows, the Holy See was compelled to relax its strict insistence that all religious should take solemn vows. One step the Church took to meet this situation was the suspension of the effects of solemn vows.[15] In addition, the Holy See began to realize the vast possibilities for good which would result from the work of Congregations whose members professed simple vows. Conditions both in Europe and in the Americas called for institutes which would devote themselves to the spiritual and corporal works of mercy—works clearly incompatible with the strict observance of the cloister. All these factors contributed to a complete change of ecclesiastical policy, and led to an attitude of positive encouragement and direct approval of Congregations that could promote and further such works.

In the early nineteenth century, such institutes began to be accorded complete formal approval without any reservations. Thus, the Congregation of the Sacred Heart of Mary obtained papal approval both for its constitutions and for the institute itself (September 14, 1821), and similar approbation was granted to the Daughters of the Sacred Heart of Jesus (November 13, 1827).[16]

---

[14] *Fontes,* n. 644.

[15] Cf. *Collectanea,* pp. 72, 86, 412, 451, 454-458, 487-489, 723-735, 736-740. It must be noted, however, that the vows of these religious, although simple in fact, were solemn *de iure,* and consequently these nuns retained their juridical status as regulars. It is well-known that there was granted a similar indult by which nuns in the United States were allowed to take simple vows.

[16] These and similar examples are listed in *Collectanea,* pp. 808-809.

The rapid multiplication of communities of this type in the nineteenth and twentieth centuries has been phenomenal. In fact, in a complete reversal of policy, the Holy See, while encouraging and approving the great increase in the number of Congregations, was and remains unwilling to approve any new Orders whose members profess solemn vows.[17] So greatly did the Church change its attitude towards religious vows that it eventually *demanded* the taking of simple vows as a preliminary to solemn profession.[18]

Although Congregations of women religious were completely approved, it should not be inferred that their members were considered religious in the strict sense. In the nineteenth century, the Sacred Congregation of Bishops and Regulars repeatedly insisted that those having only simple vows were not true religious.[19] Gradually, however, the word *"religiones"* began to be applied to Congregations professing simple vows, and the word *"religiosi,"* to their members.[20] Finally, the Code of Canon Law officially declared that "regular" and "religious" could no longer be considered synonymous, and definitively stated that those who are professed

[17] The last Order to be approved was the Order of Friars of Penance, confirmed in a brief of Pius VI (1775-1799), *Ex debito pastoralis,* March 27, 1787—*Bullarii Romani Continuatio Summorum Pontificum* (19 vols., Prati, 1835-1858), IX, 1782-1783 (hereafter cited *Bull. Rom. Cont.*). This Order was suppressed by an Apostolic Letter of Pius XI, dated November 20, 1935—*AAS,* XXVIII (1935), 482-483.

[18] S. C. Ep. et Reg., *Perpensis,* 3 maii 1902—*Fontes,* n. 2039; cf. can. 574, § 1. A similar decree had previously made the same requirement for men religious—S. C. super Statu Regularium, litt. encyc. *Neminem latet,* 19 mart. 1857—*Fontes,* n. 4381, and S. C. Ep. et Reg., decr. 19 mart. 1857—*Fontes,* n. 1976.

[19] E.g., "Instituta recentiora in quibus vota dumtaxat simplicia emittuntur haud proprie nomen religionis sibi vindicant, eorumque sodales haud proprie religiosi vocandi veniunt. . ." This, and many other similar replies to the same effect, are listed by Larraona, "Commentarium Codicis," *CpR,* I (1920), 174-186.

[20] Cf. Beat. Pius X (1903-1914), const. *Sapienti consilio,* 29 iun. 1908, I, n. 5—*Fontes,* n. 682. The *Normae,* issued by the Sacred Congregation of Bishops and Regulars on June 28, 1901, designated the members of Congregations as *"religiosi"* (nn. 58, 139, 201), but warned (n. 32) that the word *"religio"* was not to be applied to such institutes—*Normae, apud* Schaefer, *De Religiosis,* pp. 1102-1135.

with simple vows are religious in the strict canonical sense of the word.[21]

Section 2. Religious Congregations of Men

It has been seen that St. Pius V felt that abuses could best be corrected through a return to the old approval forms of the religious life, rather than through the creation of any new forms. Only two years after hs Constitution *Circa pastoralis* had suppressed Congregations of women religious with simple vows, he considered it necessary to pass a similar decree by which men religious who had only simple vows were commanded to embrace a religious Institute, that is, one in which solemn vows were taken and which was governed in accordance with one of the approved Rules.[22] However, since this Constitution was addressed to a particular group, it did not seem to be obligatory on all Congregations of men.[23]

Of all the Orders of Clerks Regular which arose in the sixteenth century, probably the most outstanding was the Society of Jesus. This Society had a unique juridical position in the Church, inasmuch as its members were permitted to take simple vows during the long period of probation before admission to solemn vows. Such an innovation was contrary to the practice which had prevailed in the Church for centuries, and aroused the opposition of many traditionalists. Indeed there were many eminent canonists and theologians who held that solemn vows were essential to the religious state.[24] When professors, relying on this opinion, began

---

[21] Cans. 487, and 488, 1°, 2°, and 7°.

[22] Const. *Lubricum vitae genus,* 17 nov. 1568—*Bull. Rom. Taur.,* VII, 725-726.

[23] Creusen, *De Juridica Status Religiosi Evolutione* (2. ed., Romae: Apud Aedes Pontificiae Universitatis Gregorianae, 1948), p. 34; Larraona, "Commentarium Codicis," *CpR,* I, (1920), 48.

[24] Suarez (*De Religione,* Tr. VII, lib. 2, c. 14, n. 2—*Opera Omnia,* XV, 181) listed Hostiensis (†1271), Panormitanus (†1453), Felinus Sondaeus (†1503), Thomas de Vio Cajetanus (†1634), Dominicus de Soto (†1560), and Navarrus (†1586) as among the proponents of this view. For a more complete treatment of this entire question, cf. O'Neill, *The Dismissal of Religious in Temporary Vows,* The Catholic University of America Canon Law Studies, n. 166 (Washington, D. C.: The Catholic University of America Press, 1942), pp. 13-25.

to teach that those Jesuits who had only simple vows were not truly religious, Claudius Aquaviva (1543-1615), the General of the Society (1581-1615), brought the matter to the attention of the reigning pontiff, Gregory XIII (1572-1585). Gregory's answer was the Constitution *Quanto fructuosius,*[25] in which he clearly stated that all Jesuits, even those having only simple vows, were and always had been religious and should be considered and called such. Despite this clear pronouncement, opposition continued, and in the succeeding year the same pontiff settled all doubts about the legal status of the Society. After giving a complete summary of the purpose and make-up of the Society, this second Constitution[26] reaffirmed the fact that the simple vows of the Society of Jesus were, by institution of the Holy See, truly and substantially religious vows, and that members having these simple vows were truly and properly religious. To prevent any further controversy, Gregory declared that a *latae sententiae* excommunication would be incurred by anyone who reopened the dispute or who directly or indirectly contradicted anything stated in the Constitution.

Thus, for the first time in the history of the Church, simple vows were recognized as truly religious vows. This official declaration clearly removed the juridical obstacles which prevented the foundation of Congregations. Although the taking of simple vows was a privilege which was reserved to the Jesuits, a precedent was established. No longer could it be maintained that solemn vows were demanded by the very essence of the religious state.[27]

Despite the most evident intention of St. Pius V, many Congregations of men were soon approved by the Holy See.[28] With

---

[25] 1 febr. 1583—*Fontes,* n. 150.

[26] *Ascendente Domino,* 25 maii 1584—*Fontes,* n. 153.

[27] Goyeneche, "De votis simplicibus in fontibus et in doctrina in ordine ad statum religiosum constituendum" (hereafter cited "De votis simplicibus"), *Acta Congressus Iuridici Internationalis* (5 vols., Romae: Libraria Pont. Instituti Utriusque Iuris, 1935-1937), IV, 307; Schaefer, *De Religiosis,* p. 56; Bouix, *De Jure Regularium,* I, 116-122.

[28] Among the earlier Congregations which obtained full papal approval may be mentioned: The Clerks Regular for administering to the sick, approved by Sixtus V (1585-1590), ep. *Ex omnibus,* 18 mart. 1586—*Bull. Rom. Taur.,* VIII, 669-670; The Clerks Regular of the Mother of God,

the passage of time, some Congregations of men religious of simple vows were even granted the privilege of exemption.[29] The positive approval of these Congregations encouraged new foundations, and literally hundreds of institutes arose in the following centuries. Their beneficial contribution to the Church and to society soon became apparent, and called forth the highest praise of the Holy See.[30]

Although the simple vows taken in the Society of Jesus were recognized as religious vows, those taken in Congregations were still not recognized as such. Congregations of simple vows received full approbation, but their members were not to be regarded as *religious* in the proper sense; as yet these institutes were called "secular congregations."[31] The two Constitutions of Gregory XII which are mentioned above had made it possible to include the members of Congregations in the religious state, but *de facto* the Church did not do so.

In the nineteenth century, many responses of the Sacred Congregation of Bishops and Regulars indicated that Congregations of simple vows were not juridically considered to be religious institutes, even though they had been approved by the Holy See.[32]

---

approved by Clement VIII (1592-1605), const. *Ex quo divina,* 13 oct. 1595—*Bull. Rom. Taur.,* X, 227-229; The Poor Clerks of the Mother of God of Pious Schools, approved by Paul V (1605-1621), const. *Ad ea,* 6 mart. 1617—*Bull. Rom. Taur.,* XII, 382-385.

29 The Congregation of Discalced Passionists, by Clement XIV (1769-1774), const. *Supremi apostolatus,* 16 dec. 1769—*Bull. Rom. Cont.,* VII, 75-79; the Congregation of the Most Holy Redeemer, by Pius VI (1775-1799), const. *Sacrosanctum apostolatus,* 21 aug. 1789—*Bull. Rom. Cont.,* X, 2111-2115; the Congregation of Pious Workers, by Pius VI, const. *Inter multiplices,* 14 dec. 1792—*Bull. Rom. Cont.,* X, 2569-2570.

30 Cf. Pius IX (1846-1878) ep. encyc. *Ubi primum,* 17 iun. 1847—*Collectanea,* pp. 868-869, and the beautiful eulogy of Blessed Pius X (1903-1914) in the opening paragraph of his Motu Proprio *Dei providentis,* July 16, 1906—*Acta Sanctae Sedis* (41 vols., Romae, 1865-1980), XXXIX (1906), 344-346 (hereafter cited *ASS*); *Fontes,* n. 675.

31 Schaefer, *De Religiosis,* p. 55, note 47; Pejška, *Jus Canonicum Religiosorum,* p. 11, note 2.

32 As stated above, in the treatment of Congregations of women, a number of such responses are given in Larraona, "Commentarium Codicis," *CpR,* I (1920), 174-176.

Pius IX (1846-1878) was unwilling to designate as true religious even those who had professed simple vows in a religious Order wherein they were eventually to profess solemn vows.[33] Even in the beginning of the twentieth century, the terminology used by the Roman Curia was not yet crystalized. The Constitution *Conditae a Christo* of Leo XIII (1878-1903)[34] gave to institutes whose members were professed with simple vows a permanent and specific standing in the common law of the Church, but did not explicitly make them an integral part of the religious state. It was not until the publication of the Code of Canon Law that all Congregations professing simple vows were admitted among religious institutes in the strict sense.[35]

Article II. Societies of the Common Life

The preceding article has recounted how the Church adhered tenaciously to its demand that all religious take solemn vows. Paradoxically, the very insistence on this strict policy was to become a contributory factor in the establishment of religious societies which would have even weaker bonds of union than obtained in Congregations of simple vows. Since the foundation of new religious institutes was a *causa maior* reserved to the Holy See, and since Congregations of simple vows could not obtain official approval, there seemed to be no juridical possibility of initiating societies with less strict obligations than such as derived from solemn vows.

The only alternative was the establishing of societies which would closely resemble religious institutes, but which lacked one

---

[33] *Collectanea*, p. 745, note; cf. Goyeneche, "De votis simplicibus," *Acta Congressus Iuridici Internationalis*, IV, 309-310.

[34] 8 dec. 1900—*Fontes*, n. 644.

[35] Cf. the explicit declaration of Pius XII (const. ap. *Provida Mater Ecclesia*, 2 febr. 1947—AAS, XXXIX [1947], 116-117): "After the Code of Pius and Benedict, . . . wisely perfecting the work begun by Leo XIII of happy memory in his immortal Constitution *Conditae a Christo*, had admitted congregations of simple vows among religious Institutes in the strict sense..." (translation taken from Bouscaren, *The Canon Law Digest* (2 vols. and Supplement through 1948, Milwaukee: The Bruce Publishing Co., 1934, 1943, 1949), Supplement, p. 66 (hereafter cited *Digest*).

of the qualities essential to the religious life as recognized by law. In this way there arose a new form of religious life which did not require its members to take public vows. This new type of society, while well adapted to the needs of the time because of its greater simplicity and freedom, did not have all the essential elements of a true religious institute, and consequently its foundation could not be said to be a violation of the law prohibiting the establishment of new religious Orders. Although some earlier groups (v.g., the Brothers of the Common Life) had already adopted this form of life, it was only from the sixteenth century onward that there began to appear on a large scale societies which imitated religious in so far as they lived in common and strove after perfection under the guidance of their own proper Constitutions, but which did not bind their members by the profession of public vows received in the name of the Church.

The immediate cause of the foundation of the first Societies of the Common Life was the reform proposed by the Council of Trent. In particular, the decrees of the Council which called for the establishment of seminaries and for the reform of the clergy[36] had a direct influence on the rise of this new type of society. At the very time the Council of Trent was in session, the Apostle of Rome, St. Philip Neri (1515-1595), began the custom of giving conferences to the clergy of the city and of providing spiritual exercises for them. Soon a regular group of priests formed a sort of company and placed themselves under the direction of the Saint. In this way was begun the Company of the Oratory, which was approved by Gregory XIII in 1575.[37] St. Philip had no intention of founding a new religious Order, and clearly indicated his desire that no vows were to be taken in his community. The final Constitutions of the Oratory, approved by Paul V (1605-1621),[38] explicitly stated that no vows or oaths or promises were taken, and that they were not to be imposed upon the members in the fu-

---

36 Conc. Trident., sess. XXIII, *de ref.*, c. 18.

37 Bulla *Copiosus,* 15 iul. 1575—*Bull. Rom. Taur.*, VIII, 541-544.

38 Bulla *Christifidelium quorumlibet,* 24 febr. 1612—*Bull. Rom. Taur.*, XII, 36-57.

ture.[39] With the advice of St. Philip, St. Charles Borromeo (1538-1584) established a similar group of secular priests, who were to assist him in a special way in caring for the varied needs of his archdiocese. These Oblates of St. Ambrose (later called the Oblates of St. Charles) took only a simple vow of obedience in the presence of the Archbishop of Milan.

One of the most outstanding Societies of the Common Life is the Congregation of the Mission (members of which are known as Vincentians or Lazarists), founded by St. Vincent de Paul (1581-1660). Full approval having been granted to its Constitutions in 1655,[40] this society was originally devoted to the work of giving missions to the poor, and later assumed the direction of seminaries. The priests of the Congregation of the Mission took *private*[41] vows of poverty, chastity, obedience, and stability, but these vows were not formally accepted either by the Church or by the community; the Congregation was officially recognized as a group of secular priests rather than as a religious body.[42] The important work of training clerics for the priesthood was the main purpose of other Societies of the Common Life, such as the Sulpicians (founded by Father Olier [1608-1657] in 1642), the Eudists (founded by St. John Eudes [1601-1680] in 1643), and the Society of Secular Clerics Living in Common (founded by Venerable Bartholomew Holzhauser [1613-1658] in 1643).

The way of life followed in Societies of the Common Life was also found to be most suitable for institutes dedicated to missionary work. In fact, the great majority of clerical societies founded in the nineteenth and twentieth centuries for the work of conversion

---

[39] Cap. IV—*ibid.*, pp. 40-41.

[40] Alexander VII (1655-1667), Breve *Ex commissa Nobis,* 22 spet. 1655 —*Bull. Rom. Taur.*, XVI, 67-69.

[41] Although the word "private" with reference to vows had not as yet been adopted by canonists, it is quite clear that the vows taken in this society corresponded to what we now call private vows. Cf. Ristuccia, *Quasi-Religious Societies,* pp. 22-24, and Stanton, *De Societatibus,* pp. 47-48, 61-62.

[42] "... utque dicta Congregatio non censeatur propterea in numero Ordinum religiosorum, sed sit de corpore cleri saecularis."—Alexander VII, Breve *Ex commissa Nobis,* 22 sept. 1655 (*Bull. Rom. Taur.,* XVI, 68).

and evangelization do not require their members to take the three public vows of religion. Among the more well-known of these societies may be mentioned the following: the Pallotine Fathers,[43] the Precious Blood Fathers, the Paris Foreign Mission Society, the Josephites, the Columban Fathers, and the Maryknoll Missioners.

It must be noted that all the societies mentioned, although belonging to the same canonical category, differ greatly among themselves. Lack of uniformity is especially noticeable in the means by which members are incorporated into the various societies. Even though these institutes are sometimes called "Societies without vows," it must be clearly understood that *public* vows are meant; actually, some of the Societies of the Common Life[44] take the same three vows as religious, the only difference being that the vows taken in Societies are *private* vows, which are not officially received in the name of the Church. In most of the Societies of the Common Life, no vows—not even private vows—are taken. Thus the Mill-Hill Fathers, the Columban Fathers, the White Fathers, and the Maryknollers take oaths instead of vows. Members of other Societies (e.g., the Eudists, the Pallotines, and the Paulists) make promises. In still other Societies (e.g., the Congregation of the Oratory, and the Society of St. Sulpice), the bond of stability is so loose that members are not required to pronounce either vows or oaths, or to obligate themselves under any form of solemn promise.[45]

The Code of Canon Law gave definite juridical recognition to Societies of the Common Life as a distinct type of society in the Church. In a special supplement to the legislation on religious[46] the Code set down specific provisions under which the new type of society is to be ruled. Canon 673 explicitly states that a Society of the Common Life is not a religious organization properly

---

[43] This Society has recently (1947) reassumed its original name: "The Society of the Catholic Apostolate."

[44] E.g., the Vincentians and the Daughters of Charity.

[45] Stanton, *De Societatibus*, pp. 96-97.

[46] Book II, Title XVII: cans. 673-681.

so-called, and that its members are not to be called religious in the strict sense of the term.[47]

The Code did not declare the exact position of these Societies in regard to the canonical state of perfection. Certainly, when it is pointed out that they are included under the general heading *"De Religiosis,"* that they are governed in part by the legislation for religious, and that they are dependent upon the Sacred Congregation of Religious, it can be concluded that the Church clearly intended to distinguish them from ordinary Associations of the faithful. Yet the present writer does not think it correct to state that Societies of the Common Life are included in the canonical state of perfection.[48] One author makes the statement that they belong not to the public, canonical state, but rather to the semi-public, juridic state of perfection.[49] Perhaps the best way to describe their status is to give the exact words of the Holy Father. In his Apostolic Constitution *Provida Mater Ecclesia,* Pius XII stated that

"... the Church with ever increasing strictness was willing to recognize this canonical state of perfection only in societies which were erected and governed by herself, that is, in religious Institutes (can. 488, 1°)... These requirements are laid down so strictly and absolutely in the Code of Canon Law, that in no case, not even by way of exception, is the canonical state of perfection recognized, unless its profession is made in a religious Institute approved by the Church."

To apply this principle to the Societies of the Common Life, the Holy Father makes this qualified statement:

"In this title (Title XVII of Book II), the Church declares *as in a fairly complete sense equivalent to the canonical state of perfection,* certain societies, ... which, though they lacked some of the

[47] "... non est proprie religio, nec eius sodales nomine religiosorum proprie designantur."

[48] The writer makes this statement despite the elaborate arguments to the contrary offered by Lauwers, "Societates sine votis et status canonicus perfectionis," *Ephemerides Theologicae Lovanienses* (Lovanii, 1924—), XXVIII (1952), 59-89, 215-238 (hereafter this article will be cited "Status canonicus," and this periodical, *ETL*).

[49] Gutiérrez, "Comparatio," *De Institutis Saecularibus,* I, 296-298.

requirements which are necessary for the complete state of perfection, . . . yet in other respects which are regarded as essentials of the life of perfection, bear a close similarity to religious Institutes and are almost necessarily connected with them."[50]

Scholion. Proper Designation of These Societies

Various names have been used to denote those societies which are governed by Title XVII of the Second Book of the Code of Canon Law. Before the Code, such societies were often called "Secular Congregations,"[51] and this terminology has been retained by some modern authors.[52] However, as Vermeersch (1858-1936) pointed out,[53] this designation was confusing, since the same name was also applied by pre-Code authors to Congregations of simple vows.[54] The Code of Canon Law did not assign any official designation to these societies; title XVII of the Second Book of the Code gives a description, rather than a name.[55]

Among modern authors, Creusen seems to be alone in using the name "Religious Societies".[56] The term, "Societies without vows," while sufficient to differentiate these societies from religious institutes in the strict sense, does not seem to distinguish them adequately from secular Institutes.[57] The title most commonly used

---

50 *AAS,* XXXIX (1947), 116-117 (translation taken from Bouscaren, *Digest,* Supplement, pp. 66-67. The italics have been added by the present writer.

51 Schaefer, *De Religiosis,* p. 989; "Traité des congrégations séculières," *Analecta Juris Pontifici* (Romae, 1855-1869; Parisiis, 1872-1891), V (1861), 52-103, 147-217.

52 E.g., Chelodi, *Jus Canonicum de Personis,* p. 465.

53 "De status religiosi essentia et interpretatio can. 487 et 488," *Periodica,* XV (1926), 8, note 1.

54 Cf. *supra,* p. 62. It is important to note that the article in the *Analecta Juris Pontifici* cited above considered societies without vows and Congregations of simple vows to be on a juridically equal basis.

55 Viz., De societatibus sive virorum sive mulierum in communi viventium sine votis.

56 *Religious Men and Women in the Code,* p. 17, note 16; "Sociétés religieuses," *ETL,* XI (1934), 778-786.

57 This term is used exclusively by Rothoff, *Le Droit des Sociétés sans Voeux.* It was also used in a decree of the S. Congregation of Religious —*AAS,* XXIV (1932), 80.

at the present time is "Quasi-Religious Societies." This designation has been used in the dissertations written at this University[58] and has been adopted by many notable canonists.[59]

Although the term "Quasi-Religious" may properly be applied to *members* of such societies, the present writer believes that there has been a trend in the past few years to call the institutes themselves "Societies of the Common Life." This title, which indicates their imitation of the religious life and at the same time distinguishes them from secular Institutes, is used by some of the most recent authors.[60] In addition, the Holy See in recent years has re-

---

[58] Ristuccia, *Quasi-Religious Societies, passim;* Waters, *The Probation in Societies of Quasi-Religious,* The Catholic University of America Canon Law Studies, n. 306 (Washington, D.C.: The Catholic University of America Press, 1950), *passim;* McFarland, *Religious Vocation—Its Juridic Concept,* p. 63, note 163, and p. 84, note 204. However, Moeder (*The Proper Bishop for Ordination and Dismissorial Letters,* The Catholic University of America Canon Law Studies, n. 95 [Washington, D.C.: The Catholic University of America Press, 1935], pp. 111-113) used "Societies without vows", and Konrad (*The Transfer of Religious to Another Community,* The Catholic University of America Canon Law Studies, n. 278 [Washington, D.C.: The Catholic University of America Press, 1949], pp. 83-86) used "Societies of the common life".

[59] Schaefer, *De Religiosis,* p. 988; Beste, *Introductio in Codicem* (3. ed., Collegeville, Minn.: St. John's Abbey Press, 1946), p. 460 (hereafter cited *Introductio*); Cocchi, *Commentarium in Codicem Iuris Canonici ad usum scholarum* (8 vols., Vol. IV [Liber II, *De Personis,* Pars II, *De Religiosis*], 4 ed., Taurinorum Augustae: Ex Officina Libraria Marietti, 1946), IV, 238 (hereafter cited *Commentarium*); De Carlo, *Jus Religiosorum* (Tornaci: Desclée et Socii, 1950), p. 508.

[60] Vermeersch-Creusen, *Epitome Iuris Canonici* (3 vols., Vol. I, 7 ed., Mechliniae et Romae: H. Dessain, 1949), I, 634 (hereafter cited *Epitome*); Fanfani, *De Iure Religiosorum* (3. ed., Rovigo: Istituto Padano di Arti Grafiche, 1949), p. 721; Conway, "Important New Law for 'Secular Institutes'," *The Irish Ecclesiastical Record* (Dublin, 1864—), 5. series, LXIX (1947), 1011-1014 (hereafter this periodical will be cited *IER*); Gutiérrez, "Comparatio," *De Institutis Secularibus,* I, 307-310; Goyeneche, "Annotationes ad Const. Ap. 'Provida Mater Ecclesia'," *Apollinaris* (Romae, 1928—), XX (1947), 29 and 35 (hereafter this article will be cited "Annotationes"); Larraona, "Constitutionis 'Provida Mater Ecclesia' pars altera," *De Institutis Saecularibus,* I, 36, 38, 39, 40, 42, 43, 56, 57, 59, 60, etc. (hereafter this article will be cited "Comment. in legem peculiarem"). The last

peatedly used the term "Societies of the Common Life."[63] For these reasons, and especially because of its growing use by the Roman Curia, the name "Societies of the Common Life" is preferred by the present writer and its use considered justified, if not compelled.

---

named author, because of his position as Secretary of the Sacred Congregation of Religious, lends an air of special authority to the use of this term.

[61] *Lex Peculiaris Institutorum Saecularium* (in const. ap. *Provida Mater Ecclesia,* 2 febr. 1947), Art. II and Art. IX—*AAS,* XXXIX (1947), 120 and 123 respectively; S. C. de Religiosis, instr. *Cum Sanctissimus,* 19 mart. 1948, n. 8—*AAS,* XL (1948), 296; S. S. de Religiosis, decr. *Cum transactis* (*de quinquennali relatione a religionibus, a societatibus vitae communis, et ab institutis saecularibus facienda*), 9 iul. 1947—AAS, XL (1948), 378-381. The last mentioned decree uses the term "*societates vitae communis*" no less than ten times within three pages.

CHAPTER III

The Rise of Secular Institutes

Article I. Historical Background

As early as the sixteenth century, attempts were made to establish institutes which deviated in some way from the traditional pattern of the religious life. According to the original intention of St. Angela Merici (1474-1540), the Ursulines were to be a group of consecrated women who would live in the world without professing vows or wearing a distinctive habit.[1] In the same way, St. Francis de Sales (1567-1622) wished to establish the Order of the Visitation as a religious community without vows or cloiter; it was only with the greatest relucance that he was prevailed upon to allow the introduction of the obligations of the cloister and of solemn vows.[2] As a result, indeed, of the determined efforts of St. Vincent de Paul (1581-1660), the Daughters of Charity were not bound to observe the cloister, but for that freedom they sacrificed the privilege of being acknowledged as religious.

The desperate conditions brought on by the French Revolution necessitated unprecedented modifications in the customary forms of the religious life. When civil law struck at the liberty and the very life of religious Orders, it was immediately recognized that new forms needed to be adopted if the religious life was to be

[1] The similarity between this group and modern secular Institutes is the subject of an article by Sister Monica, entitled "The Democratic Company of St. Angela," *Catholic World* (New York, 1865—), CLXXI (1950), 178-184. Cf. also the same author's *Angela Merici and Her Teaching Ideal* (New York: Longmans, Green and Co., 1927), especially pp. 162-164, 176, 237, 2448-249, 235-255, 287-292, 297-300, 303, 306-325.

[2] Cf. Currier, *History of Religious Orders,* pp. 419-420; Stanton, *De Societatibus,* pp. 14 and 29; Ristuccia, *Quasi-Religious Societies,* pp. 13-14; Farrell, *The Rights and Duties of the Local Ordinary Regarding Congregations of Women Religious of Pontifical Approval,* pp. 21-22.

preserved. Towards the end of the eighteenth century and during the nineteenth century, there arose societies which lacked certain elements that had previously characterized religious institutes. Some societies reduced to a minimum or excluded completely the element of the common life, and at the same time discarded all external manifestations (e.g., the religious habit) by which their members would be recognized as religious.

The most important society of this type was the Daughters of the Heart of Mary, which was very influential in preparing the way for secular Institutes. Founded by Father Pierre Joseph Picot de Clorivière, S.J. (1735-1820) in 1790, this society brought together women who wished to seek perfection while living in the world and without the obligation of wearing any distinctive dress. Even after the civil laws proscribing community life had been repealed, the Daughters of the Heart of Mary, realizing the value of a consecrated apostolate in the world, continued their original way of life. Highly praised by many French bishops,[3] this Society obtained the decree of praise from the Sacred Congregation of Bishops and Regulars on April 29, 1853, and received definitive approval four years later from the same Sacred Congregation. Final approval of its Constitutions was granted in a decree of June 18, 1890, and members of the Society (sometimes popularly called "Nardines") continue to carry on an effective apostolate today in the United States and in twenty-seven other countries of Latin America, Europe, Africa, and Asia.[4]

---

[3] Cf. the quotations given in Gambari, "Institutorum Saecularium et Congregationum Religiosorum evolutio comparata," *De Institutis Saecularibus,* I, 325, note 23 (hereafter this article will be cited "Evolutio").

[4] This Society has a privileged juridical status in the Church today. Benedict XV (1914-1922), in a letter of May 29, 1918, to the Cardinal Protector of the Society, stated that the "Constitutions of the Daughters of the Heart of Mary . . . are to be observed even in those points which differ from the prescriptions of the Code of Canon Law," and Pius XII, in a rescript of July 5, 1948, further declared that the nature of this Institute remains entirely and inviolably such as the Pontifical Decrees have recognized and approved, and that it is in no way affected by the *Provida Mater Ecclesia.* (All this information is taken from a privately printed brochure, *The Society of the Daughters of the Heart of Mary* [no

Another innovation introduced at this time was the attempt which sought to unite the benefits of the common life with the freedom of the individual apostolate. Societies of this type had two classes of members, one comprising those who lived in community, and the other made up of those who took vows while continuing to live in their own homes and carrying on their secular occupations. The "Work of Youth" founded at Marseilles in 1821 by Father Jean Joseph Allemand (1772-1836), received the decree of praise on December 5, 1863, and in this decree explicit mention was made of the fact that the majority of the members did not live in common.[5] Among other institutes whose Constitutions called for intern and extern members were the Oblates of the Sacred Heart of the Diocese of Moulins, and the Oblates of the Sacred Heart of the Archdiocese of Naples (founded in 1865 by Venerable Catherine Volpicelli [1839-1894]), which were praised by Pius IX and Leo XIII respectively for having adapted their way of life to the necessities of the times.[6]

An early organization which clearly anticipated and closely approximated secular Institutes was the Institute of the Children of Mary, founded by Father Chaminade (1761-1850) at Bordeaux about the year 1812.[7] The young men who belonged to this society took perpetual vows of obedience, chastity, and zeal. Although no vow of poverty was taken, members were required to practice the spirit of poverty, and the Constitutions explicitly stated: "No

author, publisher, or date given], pp. 29-30.) Accordingly, the Society remains a pontifically approved Congregation whose members profess simple vows even though they neither live in common nor wear a religious habit.

[5] Gambari, "Evolutio," *De Institutis Saecularibus,* I, 324, note 22; 327, note 24b. Definitively approved by Pius IX on February 24, 1871, the "Ouvre de la Jeunesse" remained a very small society and never spread outside of the diocese of Marseilles.

[6] *Ibid.,* pp. 327-328.

[7] The writer could not find any printed material regarding this society, nor is it mentioned by those few authors who have traced the historical background of secular Institutes. The fact that the existence of the society was kept secret undoubtedly explains the paucity of historical records. The information given here is the result of extensive private research in the archives of the Society of Mary by Father Gabriel Rus, S.M., to whom the present writer wishes to express his sincere gratitude.

one will keep anything, use anything, increase his revenue, except by obedience." The religious habit was worn underneath the secular garb, and members, living in their own homes, carried on an apostolate which would have been impossible for those known to be religious. There is a striking similarity between the rule composed by Father Chaminade and the rules which govern secular Institutes.

Since societies of this new type resembled religious institutes in their internal administration and bound their members to the practice of evangelical perfection in a fixed and settled way, the absence of the common life and of a distinct religious habit was considered juridically unimportant. According to the jurisprudence of the time, the new societies were praised and approved in the same way as were Congregations of simple vows. However, as this new type of society multiplied, a tendency arose within the Roman Curia to oppose the relaxation of the traditional and restricted concept of the religious life. Thus, in 1880, when the Archbishop of Naples asked the Holy See for approval of the Oblates of the Sacred Heart, his petition was rejected as inopportune. Likewise, when the decree of praise was sought by the Oblates of the Sacred Heart of the Diocese of Moulins, the Sacred Congregation of Bishops and Regulars replied that two obstacles prevented the granting of such a decree, viz., the lack of a religious habit, and the existence of a class of sisters who presumed to take the customary vows while living in their own homes in the world.[8]

The petition of this particular institute seems to have occasioned the celebrated decree *Ecclesia Catholica* (August 11, 1889), which was the only piece of legislation that was issued by the Holy See regarding the new societies up to the year 1947.[9] On June 22, 1888, the following *dubia* were presented to Leo XIII:

---

[8] When the Oblates modified their Constitutions to eliminate these obstacles, they received from Leo XIII, on May 1, 1888, both the decree of praise and papal approval as a Congregation of simple vows—Gambari, 'Evolutio," *De Institutis Saecularibus,* I, 332-333.

[9] A complete treatment of the preparation, content, and efficacy of this decree, based on original sources found in the Archives of the Sacred Congregation of Religious, is given by Gambari, *ibid.,* pp. 331-348.

I. Whether it is expedient for the Sacred Congregation of Bishops and Regulars to grant the decree of praise or approval to those Institutes which, in addition to sisters living in community, have other sisters, bound by simple vows (temporary or perpetual), who live in their own homes without any external sign by which they can be recognized as members of a religious institute?

II. Whether it is expedient for the same Sacred Congregation to grant the decree of praise or approval to those Institutes whose members, although living in community, have no external sign of membership in the Institute and who even seek to hide both the Institute itself and its nature?

To solve these difficulties, the Holy Father appointed three consultors to investigate the question and give their recommendations. Determined to uphold the traditional concept of the religious state (which required both the common life and the religious habit), the consultors asserted that it was inopportune and dangerous to relax the ancient discipline. They were not convinced that new forms of the religious life were demanded by the exigencies of the times, and therefore did not see any sufficient reason for permitting the introductions of any innovations. For these and other reasons, the consultors unanimously recommended that a negative answer be given to the two questions proposed.[10]

However, when the matter was referred to the Cardinal members of the Sacred Congregation, a less strict decision was handed down. Recognizing the usefulness of the new societies, but at the same time wishing to exclude any group which had the appearance of a secret society, the Cardinals gave a qualified affirmative answer to the first question, and a negative answer to the second. It was carefully stated that the affirmative reply given to the first question was to be understood in this sense: when the Sacred Congregation does praise or approve such Institutes, it intends to praise or approve them not as Religious Institutes of solemn vows,

[10] In the light of present events, it is interesting to note that the consultors admitted that, because of the state of persecution, such societies could be permitted in Poland, which at that time was subject to the oppressive rule of Russia.

nor as true religious Congregations of simple vows,[11] but only as pious Sodalities in which no religious profession in the proper sense is pronounced, and in which the vows, if any, are considered private, i.e., not public in the sense of being accepted by the legitimate superior in the name of the Church.[12] These societies, the decree continued, are praised or approved under this essential condition, that they become fully and perfectly known to their respective ordinaries and be entirely subject to their jurisdiction. The content of this decree was reducible to these propositions: 1) the new societies and their members do not possess the juridic character of religious, and, 2) societies which are secret in reference to ecclesiastical authority are not to be tolerated in the Church.

It seems that this decree was not in force for more than ten years; by the end of the nineteenth century it exercised no influence on the practice of the Sacred Congregation. Decrees of praise were granted to the Institute of the Daughters of Mount Calvary (June 20, 1900), and to the Lady Catechists (August 28, 1905), as Congregations of simple vows; a decree of July 5, 1911, granting what had previously been denied, recognized the extern sisters of the Oblates of the Sacred Heart of the Archdiocese of Naples as members of the Congregation with the same rights and privileges as those possessed by members living in community. No reference was made to the Decree *Ecclesia Catholica* either in the *Normae* of 1901 or in the Constitution *Conditae a Christo;* since the Decree was not incorporated into the Code of Canon Law, it must be said, in virtue of can. 6, 6°, to have lost all binding force.

The Code of Canon Law was intentionally silent regarding the new forms of religious life, and left it to future legislation to determine what provision should be made for them.[13] Within a few

[11] Indirectly, this decree is important because it was one of the earliest official documents to recognize Congregations of simple vows as true religious institutes.

[12] S. C. Ep. et Reg., decr. *Ecclesia Catholica, ASS,* XXIII (1889), 635.

[13] "Codex etiam Iuris Canonici consulto de his Institutis siluit, et quae pro ipsis essent constituenda, cum adhuc matura non viderentur, reliquit futurae legislationi."—Pius XII, const. ap. *Provida Mater Ecclesia,* 2 febr. 1947—*AAS,* XXXIX (1947), 119.

years, societies of this type began to flourish in Germany, Austria, Italy, Holland, Spain, and France. In receiving their applications for approval, the Holy See did not—and indeed could not—follow a consistent policy. Some societies, either because of their purely diocesan character, or because of their failure to bind their members to observe all the evangelical counsels, were rightly included among those Associations of the faithful which are treated in titles XVIII and XIX of the Second Book of the Code. Other societies, however, because of their interdiocesan organization and their complete dedication to the practice of perfection, very closely approximated Religious Institutes and Societies of the Common Life. Even the basic question of competence was not settled; matters pertaining to the new institutes were handled both by the Sacred Congregation of the Council and the Sacred Congregation of Religious.

Interest in these new forms of the religious life was promoted by an International Congress held at Salzburg in July, 1930, at which the founders or delegates of sixteen such societies were present,[14] and by a similar Congress, held at St. Gall (Switzerland) in 1938, at which twenty-five associations were represented.[15] At the International Juridic Congress celebrated in Rome in 1934, mention was made of the desirability of establishing definitely the legal status of this type of institute.[16]

Finally, in 1945, the Sacred Congregation of Religious appointed a special commission of five canonists to consider the entire question and to make recommendations.[17] The aim of this commission was three-fold: 1) to define the nature and juridic status of the new societies; 2) to issue a private instruction which the Sacred Congregation of Religious could use as a criterion for passing

[14] Creusen, "Formes Modernes de Vie Religieuse," *RCR,* VIII (1932), 2.

[15] Goyeneche, "Annotationes," *Apollinaris,* XX (1947), 26.

[16] Goyeneche, "De votis simplicibus," *Acta Congressus Iuridici Internationalis,* IV, 314-315; La Puma, "Evoluzione del Diritto dei Religiosi da Pio IX a Pio XI," *op. cit.,* IV, 203.

[17] Goyeneche, "Annotationes," *Apollinaris,* XX (1947), 27-28. The members of the commission were: Archbishop Pasetto (then Secretary of the Sacred Congregation), Father Larraona (then Under-Secretary), and Fathers Creusen, Grendel, and Goyeneche.

judgment on these societies, and 3) to issue norms for their erection and approval. When the members of the commission completed their work, they expressed the hope that the document, because of its importance, would be issued in the more solemn form of a *Motu proprio,* rather than by way of a simple decree. The Holy Father, who had taken a personal interest in all the work of preparation, decided to express his approval in an even more solemn way by publishing the document in the form of an Apostolic Constitution. On March 29, 1947, Pius XII promulgated the *Provida Mater Ecclesia* (under date of February 2, 1947), in which he did for secular Institutes what Leo XIII had done by his Constitution *Conditae a Christo* for Congregations of simple vows. Almost simultaneously with this Constitution, a special Commission for secular Institutes was established.[18] Within a year the Holy Father issued a *Motu proprio* praising and confirming secular Institutes,[19] and only seven days later the Sacred Congregation of Religious issued an Instruction "for the solid initial establishment and regulation of secular Institutes."[20] The extraordinary dispatch with which these documents were issued is in itself a clear indication of the Holy See's recognition of the value and importance of secular Institutes as an effective means of furthering the apostolate in the modern world.

Article II. Outline of the History and Nature of the Most Prominent Secular Institutes

As an introductory remark, the statement should be made that the present writer considers it neither necessary nor possible to give a complete account of even the most prominent secular Institutes. The very *raison d'être* of the secular character of these Institutes is the desire to make it possible for their members to influence spheres of life which are inaccessible to priests and reli-

---

[18] S. C. de Religiosis, decr. 25 mart. 1947—*AAS,* XXXIX (1947), 131-132; Bouscaren, *Digest,* Supplement, pp. 75-76.

[19] Pius XII, motu propr. *Primo feliciter,* 12 mart. 1948—*AAS,* XL (1948), 283-286; Bouscaren, *Digest,* Supplement, pp. 76-80.

[20] S. C. de Religiosis, instr. *Cum Sanctissimus,* 19 mart. 1948—*AAS,* XL (1948), 293-297; Bouscaren, *Digest,* Supplement, pp. 80-86.

gious; if members were to be recognized as belonging to officially sanctioned ecclesiastical groups, the effectiveness of their particular apostolate would be seriously impaired, if not completely destroyed. Accordingly, the Church recognizes and seeks to protect the right of members of secular Institutes to keep their identity secret.[21]

Because of this desire to maintain secrecy and also because of the comparatively recent origin of secular Institutes, there is very little printed material on the subject, except such articles as treat of Institutes in the most general terms.[22] The standard canonical commentaries which appeared before 1947 are of little value with regard to this subject.[23] Consequently, if the pages herein following

---

[21] It is incorrect to designate secular Institutes as "secret societies," since they are obliged to make known their existence to ecclesiastical authorities. However, according to a rescript of the Sacred Congregation of Religious (dated July 24, 1947), ordinaries and others who have a right, *ex officio*, to be informed of the existence of these Institutes are obliged to preserve secrecy regarding their houses, works, and members. The text of this rescript, with a short commentary, is given by Larraona, "De secreto a Superioribus ecclesiasticis circa Instituta servanda," *De Institutis Saecularibus*, I, 188-190.

[22] Probably the first bibliography which treated *ex professo* of secular Institutes was that complied by Field, *Guidance and Vocational Choice with Special Reference to the Single Life* (Typewritten Master's Dissertation: The Catholic University of America, Washington, D.C., 1951), pp. 81-85. This has apparently served as the basis of the bibliographies given in *Secular Institutes* (London: Blackfriars Publications, 1952), pp. 128-131, and in *Proceedings of the Conference on Secular Institutes* (ed. Joseph E. Haley [Chicago: Fides Publishers, 1952]), pp. 58-62.

[23] The following recent canonical works make at least some mention of secular Institutes: Vermeersch-Creusen, *Epitome*, I, 634-635; Cocchi, *Commentarium*, IV, 245-250; Jone, *Commentarium in Codicem Iuris Canonici* (2 vols., incomplete, Paderborn: Officina Libraria F. Schöningh, 1950-1952), I, 596-604 (hereafter cited *Commentarium*); De Carlo, *Jus Religiosorum*, pp. 516-518; Fanfani, *De Iure Religiosorum*, pp. 719-726; Regatillo, *Interpretatio et Iurisprudentia Codicis Iuris Canonici* (Santander: Sal Terrae, 1949), pp. 211-216; Woywod, *A Practical Commentary on the Code of Canon Law* (revised by Callistus Smith, revised and enlarged edition, 2 vols., New York: Joseph F. Wagner, Inc., 1948), I, 339-341; II, 825-830 (hereafter cited *Commentary*); Bouscaren-Ellis, *Canon Law* (2. rev. ed., Milwaukee: The Bruce Publishing Co., 1951), pp. 332-344; Abbo-Hannan, *The Sacred Canons* (2 vols., St. Louis: B. Herder Book Co., 1952), I, 686-687.

are not documented by means of authoritative sources, the reason lies in the fact that much of the material has been based on conversations with members of secular Institutes and on personal correspondence. The present writer, while fully realizing the necessity of secrecy regarding *individual members,* feels that it is desirable and in keeping with the mind of the Holy See to give some publicity to the fact that such Institutes exist in the Church today.

The Sacerdotal Society of the Holy Cross and the Work of God (usually called simply *Opus Dei*) was founded in Madrid on October 2, 1928, by Monsignor Jose Maria Escriva de Balaguer. Since that time it has spread rapidly, and now has more than one hundred houses in the various nations of Europe, Africa, and North, Central, and South America, including one in Chicago. *Opus Dei* was originally established as an Institute for men, being divided into clerical and lay groups. The women's branch, started in 1930, is absolutely separated from the men's branch and seems, in fact, to constitute a completely different Institute with its own hierarchical government. The specific aim of the *Opus Dei* is the christianization of *professional* life, while its general purpose is the sanctification of its members through the practice of the evangelical counsels. The process of beatification has already been begun for one of its members, Isidoro Zorzano, who died in 1943. *Opus Dei* has suffered many juridical vicissitudes; founded as a Pious Union, it was later recognized as a Society of the Common Life, and by a decree of the Sacred Congregation of Religious dated June 16, 1950, became the first secular Institute to receive final pontifical approval.[24]

The Company of St. Paul, begun in Milan as a Catholic Action group, later lived in community under a rule of life, and received the approval of Cardinal Ferrari (1850-1921) on November 17, 1920. At the end of three years, it became directly dependent on the Holy See, by the express wish of Pius XI. The Constitutions of the Company were approved on July 1, 1942, and on June 30, 1950, the Company of St. Paul received the decree of praise as a

---

[24] For a popular article which gives some information on this Institute, cf. Thorman, "Opus Dei," *St. Anthony Messenger* (Cincinnati, 1893—), Vol. LVIII, No. 3 (August, 1950), pp. 17-19, and 23.

secular Institute of pontifical status. Desiring to assist in the establishment of the reign of Christ in every field of modern society, this Institute is especially devoted to the apostolate of the spoken and written word.[25]

Composed of clergy, laymen, and women, the Company of St. Paul has an organized community life, although members are often given permission to live separately in the world, even for long periods of time. Each of the three separate divisions has its own Superior (called the Secretary General), who is elected by members of his particular group; the entire Company is presided over by a Superior General, who is always elected from the ranks of the clerical branch. Members are required to make a novitiate of two years in complete seclusion from the world before they take the three private ("social") vows. At the present time the Company of St. Paul is active mainly in Italy and in Argentina.

The largest secular Institute in existence today is the Institute of the Missionaries of the Kingship of Christ, which numbers more than 6500 members. Founded in Assisi on November 19, 1919, this group has had the benefit of the guidance of the well-known and learned Franciscan, Father Agostino Gemelli. The young women who compose this Institute are all members of the Third Order Secular of St. Francis. After a probation of six months and a two-year period of aspirancy, members take a vow of chastity and make the promises of poverty, of obedience, and of dedication to the apostolate; this vow and these promises are renewed annually with the intention of perpetuity. Without any form of the common life, this Institute requires its members to exercise their apostolate in the trade or profession which they practiced before entering the Institute. The Missionaries of Christ the King are active in 120 dioceses in Italy, and have been requested by the Holy Father to work in missionary countries.[26]

---

[25] An account of a somewhat unusual form of the apostolate carried on by a member of the Company in this country is given by Farina, "Miss Morris Makes a Movie," *The Lamp* (New York, 1903—), Vol. XLIX, No. 5 (May, 1951), pp. 20-22, and 30. The Miss Morris who is the subject of this article has kindly supplied the present writer with an abundance of information about the Company.

[26] This Institute has not yet been canonically established in the United

An Institute which has several unique features is that of the Schoenstatt Sisters of Mary of the Catholic Apostolate. Founded in Germany on October 1, 1926, by a Pallotine priest, Father Joseph Kentenich, this Institute is part of the highly organized Apostolic Movement of Schoenstatt, which has survived and even thrived on persecution.[27] Unlike members of other secular Institutes, the Sisters of the Catholic Apostolate wear a distinctive garb,[28] but are ready at any time to comply with the command of their Superiors to assume secular dress and live as externs in the world.[29] Another unique characteristic of this Institute is that its members do not take any vows; they are incorporated into the Institute through a solemn act of consecration, which has the force of a contract, revocable at the will of the member.[30] Composed of 1900 members throughout the world,[31] this Institute received the decree of praise on October 18, 1948,[32] and now has two houses in this country.

The Institute of St. Teresa devotes itself to the Christian edu-

---

States, but Father Stephen Hartdegen, O.F.M., of Holy Name College, Washington, D.C., is very interested in beginning an American foundation.

[27] Several branches of this Movement were founded in the concentration camp of Dachau. A complete account of the Schoenstatt Movement in general and of the Sisters of Mary in particular is given in a booklet by Sister M. Hildegarda, *The Apostolic Movement of Schoenstatt and the Schoenstatt Sisters of Mary of the Catholic Apostolate* (Cape Town, South Africa: The Standard Press, 1949) (hereafter cited *Schoenstatt*).

[28] Even though the Sisters insist that this is not a religious habit, its use must be considered a special privilege, since the usual rule is that members of secular Institutes are not to wear a uniform dress; cf. Pius XII, motu propr. *Primo feliciter,* 12 mart. 1948, n. III—*AAS,* XL (1948), 285, and S. C. de Religiosis, instr. *Cum Sanctissimus,* 19 mart. 1948, n. 7—*AAS,* XL (1948), 295-296.

[29] In this way, members of this Institute are able to continue their apostolate today in countries behind the Iron Curtain.

[30] Goyeneche, "Annotationes," *Apollinaris,* XX (1947), 24, note 64.

[31] O'Connor, "The Covenant of Love," *The Missionary Servant* (New York, 1928—), Vol. XXIV, No. 3 (March, 1951), p. 7.

[32] So it is stated by Sister M. Hildegarda, *Schoenstatt,* p. 59. However it is not included in the list of papally-approved Institutes given in the *Annuario Pontificio per l'anno* 1952 (Città del Vaticano: Tipografia Poliglotta Vaticana, 1952), p. 800.

cation of women. Founded by Dom Pedro Poveda de Castroverde in Oviedo, Spain in 1911, it was approved (as a Pious Union) by Pius XI (January 12, 1924) at the request of the Spanish hierarchy and government.[33] During the Spanish Civil War, the Teresians, because of their secular dress, were able to infiltrate into many of the Communist-controlled universities and hold teaching posts. Today, over 1000 members, all with university degrees, are carrying on the work of education in Spain, Italy, Portugal, Chile, Argentina, Uruguay, Peru, Bolivia, Mexico, England, Africa, and the Philippine Islands.[34] There are many who foresee the incalculable good that would result from the labors of a group of consecrated women who would dedicate their lives to the apostolate of teaching in public schools, and hope that the Teresian Institute[35] will soon be established in the United States.

Several Institutes have begun with the encouragement and guidance of various Religious Orders. Some mention should be made of the Carmelite Institute of Our Lady of Life[36] and the Dominican Institute of the Daughters of St. Catherine of Siena.[37] There are

---

[33] M.-T., B., "Une Réalisation Contemporaine: l'institution thérèsienne," *La Vie Spirituelle* (Paris, 1919—), LXXXI (July-December, 1949), 108-112. For an English translation of this article, see: "A Theresian Institute," *Life of the Spirit* (Oxford, 1947—), IV (1949-1950), 563-566.

[34] Cf. a newspaper account with the catchy, if inaccurate, title: "20th Century Nuns Wear Jewelry, Colored Dresses," *The Monitor* (San Francisco, 1858—), Vol. XCIV, No. 47 (February 8, 1952), p. 3.

[35] Technically, and *de iure,* this is not a secular Institute. Even though it has the form and the essential characteristics of secular Institutes, it has not, to the writer's knowledge, applied for approval as such. In *Secular Institutes* (p. 20), it is stated that the Teresians have obtained a papal indult to remain an Association of the faithful.

[36] Cf. Pond, "A Carmelite Lay Institute," *Life of the Spirit,* IV (1949-1950), 125-129.

[37] Cf. Deman, "Le groupe des Filles de Sainte Catherine de Sienne," *La Vie Spirituelle,* LXXVIII (January-June, 1948), 471-476; translation by Barbour, "The Daughters of St. Catherine of Siena," *The Torch* (New York, 1916—), Vol. XXXII, No. 9 (November, 1948), pp. 23-26.

very many other Institutes,[38] which, for reasons either of prudence or of brevity, cannot be mentioned in this study.[39]

It is hoped that the summary given here of the principal Institutes will be sufficiently indicative of the nature, purpose, and usefulness of secular Institutes as a class. Although the way of life afforded to members of secular Institutes seems particularly well adapted to the American temperament, it must be admitted that the United States has lagged behind other countries in the promotion of this newly recognized state. It would not, however, be true to say that nothing has been done here. In many places throughout the United States, unpublicized Institutes are already in existence, and others are in the process of formation. Under the direction of Father Joseph E. Haley, C.S.C., there have been several conferences on secular Institutes; the last one, held on January 26 and 27, 1952 at Notre Dame University, was attended by almost one hundred of the clergy and laity from many sections of the United States and Canada, who were anxious to obtain additional information on the theoretical and practical aspects of this new form of the apostolate.[40] Such signs of increasing interest seem to give grounds for believing that many of "these truly providential Institutes"[41] will soon be performing an effective service for the Church and the salvation of souls in our own country.

---

[38] Father Creusen reports that, by the beginning of 1950, 95 groups had applied to the Holy See for canonical erection as secular Institutes.—"Instituts Séculiers," *RCR,* XXII (1950), 29.

[39] Accounts of Institutes not mentioned here may be found in the following articles: Boland, "The Grail Movement," *The Month* (London, 1864—), Vol. CLXII, No. 829 (July, 1933), pp. 42-51; Plus, "Une fondation hollandaise: les dames de Nazareth," *La Vie Spirituelle,* LXXVIII January-June, 1948), 463-470; Sullivan, "Lay Communities," *Commonweal* (New York, 1924—), LI (October, 1949-April, 1950), 344; O'Connor, "Secular Institutes: a new apostolate," *America* (New York, 1909—), LXXXIV (October, 1949-April, 1950), 223-225; Benedict, "New Wine in New Bottles," *St. Anthony Messenger,* Vol. LVIII, No. 10 (March, 1951), pp. 4-6; "Holy See Approves Lay Religious Group," *The Monitor,* Vol. XCII, No. 28 (September 16, 1949), p. 7. Cf. also *Secular Institutes,* especially pp. 105-127.

[40] Cf. *Proceedings of the Conference on Secular Institutes* (hereafter cited *Proceedings*).

[41] Pius XII, motu propr. *Primo feliciter,* 12 mart. 1948—*AAS,* XL (1948), 286.

PART II

Legal Commentary

CHAPTER IV

THE GENERAL CONCEPT OF SECULAR INSTITUTES

Article I. Definition of Secular Institutes

Article I of the Special Law for secular Institutes defines secular Institutes as

Societies, whether clerical or lay, whose members profess the evangelical counsels in the world, in order to attain Christian perfection and to exercise a full apostolate.[1] These words contain a concrete and descriptive definition which is analogous to those given in canons 488, 1°,[2] and 673, § 1,[3] of the Code of Canon Law. This definition sets forth: 1) the nature, 2) the purpose, and 3) the divisions of secular Institutes.

Section 1. The nature of secular Institutes

The profession of the evangelical counsels of perfection is no less necessary for members of secular Institutes than it is for members of religious institutes. A mere desire or intention of living according to the counsels would certainly be insufficient; upon entering a secular Institute, a person must bind himself by some means which will insure stability in this way of life. A more detailed account of the practical manner in which this complete consecration is effected will be given in Chapter VI, which discusses Article III of the Special Law.

---

[1] Societates, clericales vel laicales, quarum membra, christianae perfectionis adquirendae atque apostolatum plene exercendi causa, in saeculo evangelica profitentur... The text of this and of all succeeding articles of the *Lex Peculiaris Institutorum Saecularium* is contained in *AAS,* XXXIX (1947), 120-124. An English translation is given in Woywod, *Commentary,* II, 827-830, and Bouscaren, *Digest,* Supplement, pp. 70-75. The translation employed here and in the following chapters is the work of the present writer.

[2] With reference to religious institutes.

[3] With reference to Societies of the Common Life.

An essential and distinctive characteristic of secular Institutes is the profession of the evangelical counsels *in the world.* This completely secular form of life indicates at once the fundamental difference between secular Institutes and religious institutes. It is clear from the law of the Church that the religious life supposes and requires some separation from the world.[4] Members of secular Institutes, on the other hand, are required to strive after perfection while living in the midst of the world. The whole reason for the existence of these Institutes is to be found in their special and singular *secular* character;[5] their apostolate is to be exercised not only *in the world,* but, as it were, *of the world.*[6] In this respect, secular Institutes seem to bear a closer resemblance to Third Orders Secular[7] than they do to religious institutes, although it must always be kept in mind that secular tertiaries do not make the *complete* and *total* consecration which is required of members of secular Institutes.

Section 2. The purpose of secular Institutes

The final cause of secular Institutes is twofold, viz., the perfection of their members, and the complete exercise of the apostolate. Both of these purposes have an intrinsic connection with each other and with the profession of the evangelical counsels. For members of secular Institutes, the ordinary and efficacious means of acquiring personal sanctification is to be found in the work of the apostolate; members bind themselves to lead lives of poverty,

---

[4] Thus, permission to leave a religious institute permanently is given by means of an indult of *secularization.*—Cans. 638; 640, § 1; 641, § 1; 643. Separation from a religious community is spoken of as "a return to the world."—Cans. 704, § 2; 642, § 1. Cf. also cans. 585; 653; 668.

[5] "...illud prae oculis semper habendum est, quod proprius ac peculiaris Institutorum character, *saecularis* scilicet, in quo ipsorum existentiae tota ratio consistit..."—Pius XII, motu propr, *Primo feliciter,* 12 mart. 1948, n. II (*AAS,* XL [1948], 284).

[6] "Hic apostolatus Institutorum Saecularium non tantum *in saeculo,* sed veluti *ex saeculo* . . . exercendus est fideliter."—*Ibil.,* 285.

[7] Cf. can. 702, § 1: Tertiarii saeculares sunt qui in saeculo . . . ad christianam perfectionem contendere nituntur, modo saeculari vitae consentaneo, secundum regulas ab Apostolica Sede pro ipsis approbatas.

chastity, and obedience precisely for this reason: in order that they may be free from every tie which could prevent a complete dedication of themselves to the apostolate.

The Constitutions of each Institute must set forth in detail those exercises of piety and Christian self-denial which will foster and develop the spiritual life of its members. In fact, a complete program of spirituality is even more necessary in Constitutions of secular Institutes than it is in Constitutions of religious institutes, because members of secular Institutes are constantly faced with the dangers of life in the world and at the same time lack those safeguards (e.g., life in common, and the religious habit) which religious enjoy.

In the same way, it is left to the Constitution of each Institute to determine the particular area of the apostolate in which its members are to be employed. In practice, the specific aims of different Institutes can be quite diverse. Some Institutes merely impose upon their members the general obligation of exercising a Christian influence in the environment in which they live. Others have a more clearly defined apostolate, such as teaching, missionary work, social service, or parochial work.

Section 3. Divisions of secular Institutes

Secular Institutes may be either clerical or lay. Since this division is clearly an adaptation of can. 488, 4°,[8] its meaning is to be understood according to the interpretation of this canon as given by commentators. Therefore, in the opinion of many canonists,[9] an Institute would be designated as clerical if many (even though not a majority) of its members are clerics, whereas a lay secular Institute is one which is composed *primarily* of lay members. *De*

[8] [Religio clericalis est] religio cuius plerique sodales sacerdotio augentur; secus est laicalis.

[9] Schaefer, *De Religiosis,* p. 85; Coronata, *Institutiones,* I, 610, note 5; De Carlo, *Jus Religiosorum,* p. 11; Sipos, *Enchiridion Iuris Canonici* (Pécs: Ex Typographia "Haladás R. T.," 1926), p. 318, note 11; Beste, *Introductio,* p. 314; Vermeersch-Creusen, *Epitome,* I, 442; Berutti, *Institutiones Iuris Canonici* (6 vols. in 7, Vol. III, Taurini-Romae: Marietti, 1936), III, 12; Larraona, "Commentarium Codicis," *CpR,* II (1921), 284-287; Ristuccia, *Quasi-Religious Societies,* p. 66.

facto, there are in existence today secular Institutes which are composed entirely of secular priests, and entrance into such Institutes has been strongly encouraged by Pius XII.[10] Since Institutes can be either clerical or lay, the practice adopted by some popular writers of referring to all secular Institutes as "lay institutes" is inaccurate and misleading.[11]

Later articles of this Special Law[12] make it clear that Institutes are also divided into those of diocesan and those of pontifical approval; Institutes which have received the decree of praise from the Holy See have pontifical legal status.

Article II. Proper Terminology

In order that they may be properly distinguished from other common Associations of the faithful, societies which correspond to the definition given above come under the special name of Institutes, or secular Institutes.[13]

The Third Part of the Second Book of the Code[14] contains legislation for the laity and for such groups of laity as Pious Unions, Confraternities, and Third Orders.

Secular Institutes are *generically* classified among these Associations of the faithful. When a person is incorporated into a secular Institute, his canonical status is not changed; he remains in the same legal category of persons to which he belonged before his entrance into the Institute.[15] The inclusion of secular Institutes among Associations of the faithful leads to important juridical consequences, which will be discussed below. It might be added, how-

---

[10] In his allocution to the Congress on the States of Perfection, December 8, 1950—*AAS,* XXXXIII (1951), 29-30.

[11] Clancy, *Secular Institutes* (Washington, D.C.: The Canon Law Society of America, 1952), p. 5.

[12] Articles V, VI, and VII.

[13] ". . . ut ab aliis fidelium communibus Associationibus (Pars Tertia, Lib. II, C.I.C.) apte distinguantur, Institutorum seu Institutorum secularium proprio nomine veniunt. . ."—*Lex Peculiaris,* Art. 1.

[14] Cans. 682-725.

[15] On the other hand, entrance into a religious community effects a radical change; by religious profession a layman is transferred into a special canonical state with its own proper duties and privileges.

ever, that Institutes are a very particular form of Association; because of their unique character, they resemble, in many respects, religious institutes and Societies of the Common Life.

A new technical expression is added to canonical terminology with the introduction of the proper name "secular Institutes." Inasmuch as these new societies are characterized by two essential elements (viz., the profession of perfection, and life in the world), there was no little difficulty in agreeing on a name which would exactly express their nature and juridic character. Such names as "religious sodalities," "religious unions," and "secular congregations" were considered, and, for various reasons, rejected.[16]

The name "Institute" was often used before the publication of the Code to refer to communities whose members professed simple vows,[17] but since the Code officially designated these as "Congregations," the word "institute" has had no specific meaning in the common law.[18] In view of the fact that the word "institute" had once been applied to Congregations of simple vows (whose position before the Code was similar to that of secular Institutes today)[19] and since the Code uses this word in speaking of moral persons[20] (which secular Institutes must be), its use seemed to be particularly appropriate.

The new societies are properly called "secular Institutes," or simply, "Institutes."[21] The use of a qualifying adjective[22] is help-

---

16 Larraona, "Comment. in legem peculiarem," *De Institutis Saecularibus,* I, 50-51.

17 Cf. *Collectanea,* pp. 808-814. Some communities still retain this term in their own proper title, e.g., the Institute of the Brothers of the Christian Schools.

18 Even in the Code, however, the word "institute" is applied in a generic sense to religious communities and Societies of the Common Life; cf. cans. 587, § 4; 1253.

19 Inasmuch as they were encouraged, praised, and approved, without being recognized as religious in the proper sense.

20 The Code applies the word *institutum* to collegiate moral persons in cans. 333, § 1, 5°; 642, § 1, 2°; to non-collegiate moral persons in cans. 1421; 1489, §§ 1, 2, 3; 1494; 1506.

21 This term is not entirely new; some pre-Code authors used the name "Secular Institutes" to designate what are now known as Societies of the

ful in avoiding any ambiguity which might arise if the term "institute" were used by itself.[23] The particular word "secular" has been chosen to indicate in an unmistakable manner that the members of these Institutes live in the world, and are thus to be distinguished from religious.

The word "secular," like the word "world," has a twofold meaning. In the pejorative sense, it refers to human life vitiated by sin and opposed to the teaching of Christ.[24] It can also refer, as it does here, simply to ordinary, everyday human life.[25] In the Code, the word "secular" is applied to all those (whether clerics or lay persons) who live an ordinary life in the world, as opposed to those who have separated themselves from the world by religious profession.[26] The word "secular" in the context, therefore, implies what is explicuitly stated in Article II, viz., that Institutes are not religious societies in the canonical sense. It also signifies that members of Institutes remain seculars even after their incorporation into the Institute. Consequently, the use of such a catch phrase as "religious in the world" to describe members of secular Institutes "is quite wrong and can only lead to regrettable confusion."[27]

The name "secular Institute" is therefore an officially recognized, technical term which has definite juridic effects.[28] A society

---

Common Life; cf. "Instituts Séculiers," *Analecta Juris Pontificii,* XVII (1888), 424-446, 689-710; XVIII (1889), 800-827.

[22] Cf. can. 488, 2°, which designates communities of simple vows as "religious Congregations," or simply as "Congregations."

[23] Such a qualification is especially important for English-speaking canonists, who often translate the word *religio as* "religious institute."

[24] The word *saeculum* is used in this sense in can. 1353.

[25] Cf. the use of *saeculum* in cans. 585; 704, § 2; 653; 668.

[26] Cans. 110; 126; 131, § 3; 250, § 1; 297; 324; 358, § 2; 367, § 1; 457; 476, § 3; 491, § 2; 524, § 1; 631, § 1; 678; 700; 702, § 1; 804, § 1; 842; 843, § 1; 844, § 2; 876, § 1; 969, etc.

[27] Lemoine, "Commentary on the Constitution 'Provida Mater'," *Secular Institutes,* p. 71 (hereafter cited "Commentary") ; cf. Larraona, "Comment. in legem peculiarem," *De Institutis Saecularibus,* I, 50-51.

[28] Canals, "De Institutis Saecularibus," *Il Monitore Ecclesiastico* (Romae, 1876-1948; ab anno 1949: *Monitor Ecclesiasticus*), LXXIV (1949), 153 (hereafter this periodical will be cited *ME*).

cannot appropriate to itself this title, unless it possesses the essential elements demanded by law, and has been approved by the Church.[29] On the other hand, societies which seem beyond all doubt to come within the requirements laid down by this Apostolic Constitution should not and may not be left among the ordinary Associations of the faithful, but must of necessity be raised to the state and form of secular Institutes.[30]

Article III. The Nature and Binding Force of This Constitution

The last phrase of Article I declares that the societies previously described and named are subject to the norms of this Apostolic Constitution.[31] This simple statement is more completely developed in Article II, § 2, which states that secular Institutes have as their own proper law the norms of this Constitution, which constitutes for them a particular statute.[32] These norms are entitled *Lex Peculiaris,* a phrase which the present writer renders as a "Special Law."[33] It has already been stated that secular Institutes are generically included among Associations of the faithful; the norms of this Apostolic Constitution form the proper law for that par-

[29] S. C. de Religiosis, instr. *Cum Sanctissimus,* 19 mart. 1948, n. I—*AAS,* XL (1948), 293-294.

[30] Pius XII, motu propr. *Primo feliciter,* 12 mart. 1948, nn. I and V—*AAS,* XL (1948), 284, and 286.

[31] "... atque huius Constitutionis Apostolicae normis subiiciuntur."

[32] "Instituta . . . tamquam proprio iure. . . his praescriptis reguntur: 1° Generalibus huius Constitutionis Apostolicae normis, quae omnium Institutorum saecularium veluti proprium statutum constituunt."

[33] There is no unanimity among the authors in regard to the various divisions of law; in fact, the Code itself is not completely consistent in this matter. The writer here follows those commentators who state that, with reference to territory, laws are either universal or particular; with reference to the persons who are subject to the law, they are either general or special—Van Hove, *Commentarium Lovaniense in Codicem Iuris Canonici* (Vol. I, tom. 1, *Prolegomena ad Codicem Iuris Canonici,* 2. ed., Mechliniae-Romae: H. Dessain, 1945), I, 42-43; Vermeersch-Creusen, *Epitome,* I, 20. Since these norms bind a particular class of persons (rather than all persons residing in a particular territory), the use of the term "special law" seems preferable to the term "particular law."

ticular species of Association which is known as a secular Institute. In another respect, the *Lex Peculiaris*—despite its name—can be said to be a common and general law, because it contains the essential notes which are common to all secular Institutes.

The importance of this Special Law may be brought out more clearly by a discussion of its relationship to the legislation contained in the Code. According to canon 22, a more recent law passed by a competent authority abrogates a former law, if the new law explicitly says so, or if it is directly contrary to the former law, or if it readjusts the entire subject matter of the former law.[34] In the present case, the new law contains an explicit and forceful derogatory clause.[35] It seems certain that, in those matters which are mentioned in the *Lex Peculiaris,* the legislator has manifested his intention of readjusting entirely the former law. In so far as this law decrees what is contrary to the law of the Code, it constitutes a tacit revocation of the former law. Consequently, from all three points of view, the *Lex Peculiaris* must be said to prevail, when it conflicts with the provisions of the Code.

In accordance with the principle of law: *generi per speciem derogatur,*[36] secular Institutes are not bound by those laws for Associations of the faithful which are contrary to their own Special Law; they can and must follow their own proper law completely. On the other hand, Institutes have not been completely withdrawn from the category of secular Associations, and are subject to their law in any matter that is not contained in the *Lex Peculiaris,* or that is not contrary to it.

Finally, a word must be said about future legislation. The second principle enunciated in canon 22 applies here: A general law by no means abolishes the particular law of places and persons,

---

[34] Lex posterior, a competenti auctoritate lata, obrogat priori, si id expresse edicat, aut sit illi directe contraria, aut totam de integro ordinet legis prioris materiam...

[35] "... contrariis quibuslibet non obstantibus, peculiarissima etiam mentione dignis..."—Article X.

[36] Reg. 34, R.J., in VI°.

unless it expressly decrees otherwise.[37] Accordingly, a future general law regarding Associations of the faithful will not derogate from the provisions of the *Lex Peculiaris*, unless this future law explicitly states such a derogation.

---

[37] . . . firmo praescripto can. 6, n. 1, lex generalis nullatenus derogat locorum specialium et personarum singularium statutis, nisi aliud in ipsa expresse caveatur. Cf. the commentary given on this canon by Michiels, *Normae Generales Juris Canonici* (2. ed., 2 vols., Parisiis-Tornaci-Romae: Desclée et Socii, 1949), I, 654-667.

CHAPTER V

The Juridic Position of Secular Institutes

Article I. Non-Religious Character of Institutes

The brief definition contained in Article I is given further elaboration in Article II, which states explicitly what is contained in the first Article only by way of implication.

Secular Institutes do not admit the three public vows of religion (cans. 1308, §1, *and* 488, 1°), *nor do they impose upon all their members the obligation of the common life or of a common domicile, according to the canons (cans.* 487 *ff. and* 673 *ff.).*

This statement leads to the following juridical consequences:

1° *By law, according to rule, secular Institutes are not religious institutes (cans.* 487 *and* 488, 1°) *or Societies of the Common Life (can.* 673, § 1), *nor can they properly be called such.*

2° *They are not bound by the proper and special law of religious institutes or Societies of the Common Life, nor can they invoke such law, except when some provision thereof (especially of the law governing societies without public vows) may by way of exception have been legitimately adapted and applied to them.*[1]

Section I. Absence of public vows and of the common life

Although it is essential that members of secular Institutes be

[1] Instituta saecularia, cum nec tria publica religionis vota (cc. 1308, § 1, et 488, 1°) admittant, nec communem vitam seu commorationem sub eodem tecto omnibus suis membris, ad normam canonum, imponant (cc. 487 sqq. et 673 sqq.):

1° Iure, ex regula, nec sunt nec proprie loquendo dici queunt Religiones (cc. 487 et 488, 1°) vel Societates vitae communis (c. 673, § 1);

2° Religionum aut Societatum vitae communis proprio peculiarique iure non obligantur neque ipso uti possunt, nisi quatenus aliquod huius iuris praescriptum, illius praecipue quo Societates absque votis publicis utuntur legitime ipsis, per exceptionem, accommodatum fuerit atque applicatum.— Article II, § 1.

bound to the profession of evangelical perfection in some fixed and abiding manner, the Church does not require them to take vows;[2] the necessary stability can be attained by other means, such as by taking oaths or promises. It is true that the Constitutions of a particular Institute may require its members to take either the vow of poverty, or of chastity, or of obedience (or even all three), but the taking of such vows is not demanded by the common law governing all Institutes. Whereas members of religious communities must profess the three vows of religion,[3] a secular Institute can receive ecclesiastical approval even though its members are not required to take any vows.

Moreover, even if vows are taken in an Institute, these vows are not recognized by the Church as public vows. As defined in the Code, public vows are those which are accepted in the name of the Church by a legitimate ecclesiastical superior; all others are private.[4] According to the positive legislation of Article II, vows taken by members of secular Institutes are not officially received in the name of the Church, and therefore must be considered private vows.

It must, however, be pointed out that when vows are taken as a means of incorporation into a secular Institute, they are not identical with those completely private vows which are taken by an individual and which pertain exclusively to the internal forum. Vows which may be taken in an Institute are juridically private, but they produce definite legal effects in such matters as submission to superiors, rights in the Institute, etc. In a sense, the Church assists at the taking of such vows (although it does not

---

[2] Cf. Chapter VI, which treats of Article III.

[3] Can. 488, 1°.

[4] Votum est *publicum,* si nomine Ecclesiae a legitimo Superiore ecclesiastico acceptetur; secus *privatum.*—Can. 1308, § 1. It may be helpful to state here that the word "public," as applied to vows, is not used in opposition to the word "occult" (cf. can. 2197, 4°). Even though public and external formalities accompany the pronouncement of a vow, the vow is not necessarily a public vow in the juridical sense.—Schaefer, *De Religiosis,* p. 53.

officially receive them)[5] and regulates them by approving the Constitutions upon which they are based. Inasmuch as these vows have a recognized relationship to the external forum, the designation of them as "private vows" seems misleading. In order to distinguish them more accurately from vows which refer completely to the internal forum, the vows taken in secular Institutes can be called "recognized private vows."[6] In the opinion of the present writer, the term "semi-public vows"[7] or "social vows"[8] expresses more precisely the nature of vows taken in secular Institutes.

The unique nature of secular Institutes is further elucidated by the statement that the observance of the common life is not obligatory on their members. The profession of perfection does not seem to require, *ex rei natura,* the element of the common life,[9] but in virtue of the positive legislation of the Church this element is today essential for the religious state.[10]

The notion of the common life can have a twofold meaning. In the formal sense, it signifies incorporation into a society which, being a moral person, is governed by superiors in accordance with its proper Constitutions. In the material sense, it means dwelling

---

[5] By way of analogy, the mutual consent in the Sacrament of Matrimony is not received by the Church, even though the Church requires that this consent be pronounced under certain conditions and *coram Ecclesia.*

[6] Canals, "De Institutis Saecularibus," *ME,* LXXIV (1949), 156.

[7] Idem, *loc. cit.;* Larraona, "Comment. in legem peculiarem," *De Institutis Saecularibus,* I, 58; Gutiérrez, "Comparatio," *op. cit.,* I, 306, 308; Clancy, *Secular Institutes,* p. 6. (Cf. the use of "semi-public" as applied to oratories in can. 1188, § 2, 2°.)

[8] Cf. *Proceedings,* p. 7. This term is found in the approved Constitutions of the Company of St. Paul, and was used by Father Larraona in a talk given at the Congress on the States of Perfection, as reported in *L'Osservatore Romano* (Roma, 1861-1929; Città del Vaticano, 1929—), December 1, 1950.

[9] Saurez, *De Religione,* Tr. VII, lib. 2, cap. 4, n. 4—*Opera Omnia,* XV, 128; Schmalzgrueber, *Ius Ecclesiasticum Universum* (5 vols. in 12, Romae, 1843-1845), lib. 3, tit. 31, n. 21; Bouix, *De Jure Regularium,* I, 56-64; Vermeersch, "De status religiosi essentia et interpretatione can. 487 et 488," *Periodica,* XV (1926), 5; Wernz-Vidal, *Ius Canonicum,* III, 9; Schaefer, *De Religiosis,* p. 58; Fanfani, *De Iure Religiosorum,* pp. 1-2.

[10] Can. 487.

together under the same roof and sharing with others in the ordinary needs of life, such as food and clothing.[11] Common life as understood in the formal sense is a juridically essential element of the religious state; according to the norms of law in force at the present time, the private and individual profession of perfection (such as, for example, that made by a hermit) lacks canonical recognition.[12] Moreover, once the bond by which a person is incorporated into a religious society is broken, that person *ipso facto* ceases to be a religious.[13]

The observance of the common life in the material sense is imposed by law on religious as a general rule,[14] but cannot be said to be absolutely essential. Thus, apostates and fugitives from the religious life,[15] those who have received an indult of exclaustration,[16] and religious who have been promoted to the episcopacy[17] do not live a community life, and yet they retain their status as religious. In the same way, the obligation of observing the common life (in both the formal and the material sense) is binding in Societies of the Common Life; in fact, this is the distinctive and characteristic element from which these Societies derive their proper name.

Since only the *social* profession of perfection receives legal recognition, it is clear that in approving secular Institutes the Church requires their members to observe the common life in the formal sense; incorporation into an Institute is obviously necessary. On the other hand, the unique nature of secular Institutes demands a certain amount of freedom, and in many cases the obligation of community life would constitute an obstacle to the work of the apostolate. Accordingly, the Special Law does not impose this obligation as an essential requirement of all Institutes, but leaves

---

11 Bouscaren-Ellis, *Canon Law*, pp. 229-230; Larraona, "Commentarium Codicis," *CpR*, II (1921), 138; Maroto, "Consultationes," *CpR*, V (1924), 244.

12 Schaefer, *loc. cit.;* Coronata, *Institutiones*, I, 605.

13 Can. 640, § 1.

14 Cf. cans. 487; 587, § 2; 594, § 1; 606; 638; 2389, etc.

15 Can. 645, § 1.

16 Can. 639.

17 Cans. 627 and 629.

each group free to determine what will best suit its own particular character. In practice, most Institutes do not make any provisions for life in common, save in exceptional cases;[18] others require that some members live in common; still others[19] have a general rule obliging all members to observe the common life except under special, determined circumstances.

It is important to mention that even when the common life in the material sense is followed in secular Institutes, this cannot be called the common life in the strict canonical sense. Such matters as permission to enter or to leave the house, and absences and interruptions of residence are determined not by the common law of the Code, but rather by the Constitution of the particular Institute. All these matters must be adapted in such a way as to correspond to the secular nature and apostolic purpose of the Institute.

Section 2. Exclusion of law governing religious

From what has been said, it is apparent that secular Institutes lack some of the elements which are essential both to religious institutes and to Societies of the Common Life. The lack of the three public vows of religion distinguishes Institutes from religious societies as defined by law; the absence of the common life (in the material sense) distinguishes them from Societies of the Common Life. Members of Institutes have this in common with quasi-religious: they are not required by the common law to take any or all of the three vows, and such vows, if they are taken, are not juridically classed as public vows. Consequently, just as the Code declares that members of Societies of the Common Life cannot be called religious in the proper sense since they are not bound by the usual three public vows,[20] so also members of secular Institutes cannot be designated as religious in the canonical sense.[21]

---

[18] Cf., however, the prescriptions of Article III, § 4, *infra*, pp. 162-165.

[19] E.g., the Institute known as the Company of St. Paul.

[20] Can. 637, § 1.

[21] It should be noted that the Special Law qualifies the statement that secular Institutes are not and cannot properly be called religious institutes. The words *"iure, ex regula,"* allow for the possibility that the Church can, by way of exception, recognize as religious certain societies which are or-

If secular Institutes are not religious institutes or Societies of the Common Life, it is certainly fitting that they should not be bound by the norms contained in the Second Part of the Second Book of the Code (cans. 487-681). As one author remarks,[22] it would be a definite disadvantage if Institutes were obliged to follow laws which were not made for them; in many instances, a strict and literal application of the law for religious would be inconsistent with the nature and necessities of secular Institutes.[23]

As a general rule, Institutes are forbidden to appropriate to themselves the laws for religious institutes; exceptions cannot be presumed but must be proved, e.g., by the express or equivalent declaration of the legislator. Just as the law for religious (and especially that for religious Congregations) is applied in some matters to Societies of the Common Life,[24] so it is foreseen that the Church may apply some particular provisions of the common law for religious (and especially that for Societies of the Common Life) to secular Institutes. Thus, the provisions of canon 510 requiring a quinquennial report have already been extended to secular Institutes.[25]

In many cases the common law for religious may provide a directive norm for secular Institutes.[26] Whenever the regulations

---

ganized along the lines proper to secular Institutes. *De facto,* the Daughters of the Heart of Mary are acknowledged as members of a religious congregation in the canonical sense, despite the fact that they neither live in common nor wear a religious habit; cf. *supra,* p 45, note 4. A similar exception is mentioned by Piatus Montensis (Jean Joseph Loiseaux), *Praelectiones Juris Regularis* (2. ed., 2 vols., Tornaci, 1896), I, 16. It seems unlikely that such exceptions will be made after the promulgation of the *Provida Mater Ecclesia.*

22 Guay, "Ies Instituts séculiers," *Revue de l'Université d'Ottowa* (Ottawa, 1930—), XVIII (1948), p. 81* (hereafter this periodical will be cited *RUO*).

23 E.g., those canons which regulate the obligation of poverty, viz., cans. 569, 580, 583, etc.

24 Cans. 673-681.

25 S. C. de religiosis, decr. *Cum transactis,* 9 iul. 1947—*AAS,* XL (1948), 372-381.

26 E.g., the canons regulating the qualifications for (can. 504) and the duration of office (can. 505) of superiors, the canonical elections (cans.

already in force for religious communities are extended to secular Institutes, they must be adapted to the specific nature and circumstances of life in these Institutes. The phrase *congrua congruis referendo,* which appears so often in the Code,[27] must be the guiding directive in making such an accommodation.[28]

Article II. Legislation Governing Secular Institutes

The Special Law proceeds to enumerate in a positive way the various sources of legislation by which secular Institutes are to be ruled.

These Institutes, while observing the common norms of canon law which concern them, are governed by the following prescriptions as their proper law, corresponding more closely to their specific character and condition:

1° *By the general norms of this Apostolic Constitution, which constitute as it were the special statute of all secular Institutes;*

2° *By the norms which the Sacred Congregation of Religious may decide to issue, according as necessity demands or experience suggests, by way either of interpreting this Apostolic Constitution or of elaborating and applying it to all or some of these Institutes;*

506-507), the transfer of members to religious institutes or to other secular Institutes (cans. 632-636), the dismissal of members (cans. 647-671), etc. Cf. the statement contained in No. 9 of the Instruction *Cum Sanctissimus* of the Sacred Congregation of Religious, dated March 19, 1948 (*AAS,* XL [1948], 296), with reference to can. 500, § 3.

[27] E.g., in cans. 304, § 2; 609, § 1; 658, § 2; 664, § 1; 675; 681; 1995.

[28] A detailed treatment of this particular question is given in L.-G., "Iurisprudentiae pro Institutis saecularibus hucusque conditae summa lineamenta," *De Institutis Saecularibus,* I, 198-234; Heston, "The Government of Secular Institutes," *Secular Institutes,* pp. 89-104.

1° Generalibus huius Constitutionibus Apostolicae normis, quae omnium Institutorum saecularium veluti proprium statutum constituunt;

2° Normis quas Sacra Congregatio de Religiosis, prout necessitas ferat atque experientia suffragetur, sive Constitutionem Apostolicam interpretando sive ipsam perficiendo atque applicando pro omnibus vel pro aliquibus ex his Institutis edere censuerit;

3° By the particular Constitutions approved according to the following Articles (Arts. V-VIII), which may prudently modify the general rules of law and the special norms set forth above (nn. 1° and 2°) in accordance with the widely differing aims, needs, and circumstances of particular Institutes.[29]

Since secular Institutes are recognized groups of the faithful, they are subject both to the common law which governs such groups[30] and to that which binds individual members of the faithful. According to Article V, Institutes have moral personality; they are therefore bound by the general laws which regulate collegiate moral bodies.[31] Since they are not religious, but *secular,* moral collegiate persons, they are generally subject to the prescriptions of canons 684-699.[32] In the same way, since incorporation into a secular Institute does not change a person's canonical status, lay members of Institutes are subject to the prescriptions of the Code which govern the faithful, and clerical members, except for a contrary privilege, are bound by the laws for secular clerics (e.g., with regard to obligations, duties, studies, incardination, ordination, penalties, etc.). However, this general subjection to common

---

3° Particularibus Constitutionibus, ad normam Articulorum qui sequuntur (Art. V-VIII), approbatis, quae generales iuris atque peculiares supra descriptas normas (nn. 1° et 2°), singulorum Institutorum finibus, necessitatibus, adiunctis, non parum inter se diversis, prudenter accommodent. —Article II, § 2.

[29] Instituta, salvis communibus iuris canonici normis quae ipsa respiciant, tamquam proprio iure, peculari eorum naturae et conditioni arctius respondenti, his praescriptis reguntur:

[30] Many examples of this might be cited; to take only one, secular Institute are capable of introducing legal customs in accordance with the prescriptions of can. 26. Explicit treatment of this is given in Cook, *Ecclesiastical Communities and Their Ability to Induce Legal Customs,* The Catholic University of America Canon Law Studies, n. 300 (Washington, D. C.: The Catholic University of America Press, 1950), pp. 114-115.

[31] Cans. 99-107; 1494, § 2.

[32] Book II, Title XVIII, *de fidelium associationibus in genere.* The following title, *de fidelium associationibus in specie* (cans. 700-725), does not pertain to secular Institutes; the Special Law of this Apostolic Constitution takes the place of Title XIX with regard to secular Institutes.

norms is always subject to limitations arising from the Special Law or from the particular Constitutions.[33]

In some instances the common law is evidently inapplicable to groups which the legislator did not have in mind, and may even interfere with their mission; in such cases, secular Institutes must look elsewhere for their legislation. The norms of this Apostolic Constitution were drawn up to correspond precisely to the specific nature and conditions of secular Institutes and they constitute for them a proper statute. Institutes are likewise affected by later documents which complete or interpret this *ius proprium.*[34] Since the norms given here are neither complete nor definitive, it is foreseen that complementary norms will be necessary in the future.[35] For this purpose the Holy Father has given extensive powers to the Sacred Congregation of Religious,[36] which can interpret,[37] clarify, apply, and complete the norms of the Special Law, either for all Institutes or for some particular class of Institutes (e.g., clerical Institutes).

The succinct provisions of this Special Law and the general norms issued by the Sacred Congregation are certainly insufficient to provide for all the details of life in a secular Institute. Although the Code has almost two hundred canons on religious, it leaves untouched many phases of the religious life which can be better regulated by the particular Constitutions of each community. Because of the diverse nature and purpose of religious communities, it would be a practical impossibility for the common law to deter-

---

[33] Cf. *supra,* pp. 68-69.

[34] E.g., Pius XII, motu propr. *Primo feliciter,* 12 mart. 1948—*AAS,* XL (1948), 283-286.

[35] ... etsi completae atque definitivae normae Instituta Saecularia respicientes . . . in opportunius tempus melius differantur . . .—S. C. de Religiosis, instr. *Cum Sanctissimus,* 19 mart. 1948—*AAS,* XL (1948), 293.

[36] Hisce autem ut supra constitutis, ad ea omnia exsecutioni mandanda Sacram Congregationem de Religiosis deputamus, cum omnibus facultatibus necessariis atque opportunis... Pius XII, const. ap. *Provida Mater Ecclesia,* 2 febr. 1947—*AAS,* XXXIX (1947), 120.

[37] It is the opinion of the present writer that this Sacred Congregation has the right to interpret *authentically* the norms contained in this Apostolic Constitution.

mine all the minute aspects of life in every community. The Church wisely leaves each community free to make specific applications of the general law to its own special needs. *A fortiori,* one can expect that secular Institutes (which have only ten brief articles as their special law) will be ruled in large measure by their own proper Constitutions. The almost unlimited diversity among secular Institutes likewise demands that each group draw up its own particular rule of life, subject to the approval of the Church. In actual practice, the Constitutions provide the primary source of legislation, quantitatively measured, by which life in Secular Institutes is ordained.

Article III. Competence of the Roman Congregations

The question of competence is not only of practical importance, but has doctrinal implications as well. Historically, those societies which were forerunners of secular Institutes were in some instances approved by the Sacred Congregation of Bishops and Regulars, and in other instances, by the Sacred Congregation of the Council. The dispute in the matter of competence, which has persisted up to fairly recent times, is now settled by Article IV of this Special Law.

Section 1. The Sacred Congregation of Religious

Secular Institutes (Art. I) are subject to the Sacred Congregation of Religious, without prejudice to the rights of the Sacred Congregation for the Propagation of the Faith, as set down in can. 252, § 3, with reference to Societies and Seminaries destined to serve the foreign missions.[38]

The Sacred Congregation of Religious alone is competent to decide questions which affect societies that have been approved as secular Institutes. Such Institutes are clearly distinguished from other secular Associations, and are withdrawn from the jurisdic-

[38] Instituta saecularia (Art. I) a Sacra Congregatione de Religiosis dependent, salvis iuribus Sacrae Congregationis de Propaganda Fide, ad normam c. 253, §3, quoad Societates et Seminaria Missionibus destinata.—Article IV, §1.

tion of the Sacred Congregation of the Council. The exclusive competence of the Sacred Congregation of Religious is restated and confirmed both in the Motu Proprio *Primo feliciter*[39] and in the Instruction *Cum Sanctissimus.*[40]

It is important to note the reason for which the Church attributes competence to this Sacred Congregation. In the words of the Holy Father:

> "Secular Institutes, even though their members live in the world, still by reason of the full consecration to God and to souls which they profess with the approval of the Church, and by reason of the internal hierarchical, interdiocesan and universal organization which they can have in varying degrees, are according to the Apostolic Constitution *Provida Mater Ecclesia* rightly and deservedly numbered among the states of perfection juridically constituted and recognized by the Church. The Institutes have therefore deliberately been assigned and committed to the competence and care of that Sacred Congregation which is entrusted with the care and ruling *of the public states of perfection.*'"[41]

It is with wisdom and caution that the phrase "*juridic* state of perfection" is used with reference to secular Institutes; in no official document are they said to constitute a *canonical* state of perfection[42] Some authors[43] have, perhaps unguardedly,[44] called sec-

[39] V—*AAS,* XL (1948), 285-286.

[40] 2—*AAs,* XL (1948), 294.

[41] Motu propr. *Primo feliciter,* 12 mart. 1948, n. V— *loc. cit.*

[42] The very title of the *Provida Mater Ecclesia* speaks of "the canonical states of perfection and of secular Institutes," thereby implying a difference between the two. This Constitution also refers to Institutes as associations which "*approach* more closely to the canonical states of perfection" ("... quae ... proprius quoad substantiam accedunt ad status canonicos perfectionis. . .")—*AAS,* XXXIX (1947), 117-118. The translation and italics are supplied by the present writer.

[43] E.g., Carpentier, "Constitution Apostolique 'Provida Mater Ecclesia,' " *Nouvelle Revue Théologique* (Paris, 1869—), LXIX (1947), 426 (hereafter this periodical will be cited *NRT*); Bergh, "Les Instituts Séculiers," *NRT,* LXX (1948), 1052; Jombart, "Un Nouvel Etat de Perfec-

ular Institutes a new canonical state of perfection, and at least one writer[45] has gone to great lengths to prove this contention. The distinction may seem to be an extremely subtle one, but it is nevertheless important because of the legal consequences implied through the use of these terms.[46] In the opinion of the present writer, only those who are in the religious state can be said to belong to the complete, public, canonical state of perfection; members of secular Institutes belong to the incomplete, semi-public state which is most acurately termed the *juridic* state of perfection.[47]

Since secular Institutes are a legally recognized state of perfection, it is quite proper that they be entrusted to the care of the Sacred Congregation of Religious. The competence of this Sacred Congregation is exclusive, universal, and personal. Even Institutes in countries which are subject to the Sacred Congregation for the Propagation of the Faith come within the competence of the Sacred Congregation of Religious,[48] the only exception being

---

tion, Les Instituts Séculiers," *Revue d'Ascétique et de Mystique* (Toulouse, 1910—), XXIV (1948), 272 (hereafter this periodical will be cited *RAM*).

[44] Thus Jombart in a later article has explicitly stated that secular Institutes constitute a juridic state, but not a canonical state of perfection; cf. his article, "Un état de perfection au milieu du monde," *Revue de Droit Canonique* (Strasbourg, 1951—), II (1952), 66 (hereafter this periodical will be cited *RDC*).

[45] Lauwers, "Status canonicus," *ETL*, XXVIII (1952), 215-237.

[46] As Lauwers (*loc. cit.*) points out, if secular Institutes connote a canonical state of perfection, their members might well be included in the term *religiosi*, as this word is used in can. 107.

[47] Cf. the more complete treatment given by Gutiérrez, "Comparatio," *De Institutis Saecularibus*, I, 267-277, 301-306. Cf. also Larraona, "Comment. in legem peculiarem," *op. cit.*, I, 42, 45, 102; Jone, *Commentarium* I, 597; Clancy, *Secular Institutes*, p. 5; Onclin, "Chronica Actorum Sanctae Sedis," *ETL*, XXIV (1948), 457; Canals, "De Institutis Saecularibus," *ME*, LXXIV (1949), 154; Delchard, "Etat de perfection, voeux et consécration dans les instituts séculiers," *RDC*, I (1951), 281-284 (hereafter this article will be cited "Consecration").

[48] Some of the earlier commentators on secular Institutes held that the Sacred Congregation for the Propagation of Faith had competence over Institutes in missionary lands; cf. Guay, "Les Instituts séculiers," *RUO*, XVIII (1948), 91*; Carpentier, "Constitution Apostolique 'Provida Mater

that of seminaries and Societies of *ecclesiastics* which are founded exclusively for missionary purposes.[49]

The ascribing of exclusive competence to this Sacred Congregation has, in a certain sense, a retroactive effect. Societies which were founded and approved (even, e.g., by the Sacred Congregation of the Council) before the appearance of this Apostolic Constitution, if they possess the essential requirements of secular Institutes as herein described, must, in the absence of special privilege, be converted to this new form and submit to the jurisdiction of the Sacred Congregation of Religious.[50]

Section 2. The Sacred Congregation of the Council

Associations which neither have the nature nor fully profess the purpose described in Article I, and those also which lack any of the elements mentioned in Articles I and III of this Apostolic Constitution are governed by the law of Associations of the faithful (can. 684 ff.), and come under the Sacred Congregation of the Council, with a full application however of the prescriptions contained in canon 252, § 3, with reference to the territory of the missions.[51]

Ecclesia,'" *NRT,* LXIX (1947), 430; Jombart, "Un Nouvel Etat de Perfection, Les Instituts Séculiers," *RAM,* XXIV (1948), 273. This opinion is no longer tenable in view of the following declaration of the Sacred Congregation of Religious: "Associationes fidelium quae rationem notasque habent in Constitutione Apostolica descriptas, ab hac Sacra Congregatione de Religiosis omnes ubique, sive in territoriis iuris communis sive in territoriis Missionum, iure ad normam ipsius Constitutionis dependent (Art. IV, §§ 1 et 2) et Constitutionis Legi peculari subiiciuntur..."—S. C. de Religiosis, instr. *Cum Sanctissimus,* 19 mart. 1948, n. 2 (*AAS,* XL [1948], 294).

[49] Can. 252, §3; cf. also can. 252, § 5.

[50] . . . omnes societates ubique gentium—etsi ordinaria vel etiam pontificia approbatione suffultas—, cum elementa et requisita Institutorum Saecularium propria habere noscantur, ad hanc formam necessario illico redigendae sunt, . . . atque, ut directionis unitas servetur, uni S. Congregationi de Religiosis in cuius sinu Speciale de Institutis Saecularibus Officium constitutum fuit, merito attribui ac devolvi decrevimus.—motu propr. *Primo feliciter,* n. V (AAS, XL [1948], 286).

[51] Consociationes, quae rationem non habent seu plene finem non profi-

It is quite clear that this Special Law is applicable only to those societies which are *de facto et de iure* secular Institutes. Some societies, such as sodalities, which have for their purpose religious or charitable works, cannot become secular Institutes. Third Orders Secular, although they require their members to seek after perfection, do not demand that complete consecration to perfection and the apostolate which is characteristic of secular Institutes. Still other groups may possess all the essential elements enumerated in this Apostolic Constitution, but may have received approbation as Associations of the faithful. This latter group, until their recognition as secular Institutes, are governed by the common norms for Associations as found in canons 684-699.[52]

In accordance with canon 250, § 2, pious sodalities and unions —with the exception of Third Orders Secular[53]—are dependent upon the Sacred Congregation of the Council wherever the common law of the Church is in force. In missionary lands, the Sacred Congregation for the Propagation of the Faith has competence over Associations of the faithful.[54]

---

tentur in Art. I descriptum, illaeque etiam, quae aliquo ex elementis carent in Art. I et III huius Constitutionis Apostolicae recensitis, iure reguntur Associationum fidelium, de quibus in cc. 684 sqq. et a Sacra Congregatione Concilii dependent, salvo praescripto c. 252, § 3, quoad territoria Missionum.—Art. IV, §2.

[52] Existing societies which have all the essential elements of secular Institutes must apply for recognition as such (cf. the text given above in footnote 50). However, it is the express wish of the Holy See that such societies prove themselves and evolve gradually (*"pedetemptim atque per gradus"*) through the various forms of secular Associations before seeking the honor of approval as secular Institutes. In this way will be avoided the indiscriminate and imprudent establishment of groups which have little or no hope of permanent success. Cf. instr. *Cum Sanctissimus,* nn. 5 and 6 —*AAS,* XL (1948), 294-295.

[53] These are subject to the Sacred Congregation of Religious—can. 251, § 1.

[54] Can. 252, § 2.

CHAPTER VI

Essential Elements of Secular Institutes

Article III, which lays down what is required by the Holy See before an Association can be erected into a secular Institute, is the most important Article contained in the Special Law.[1] Associations which do not certainly possess the requisites prescribed in this Article cannot be included among the states of perfection; such societies, no matter how fervent, meritorious, and useful to the Church they may be, must be left, at least provisionally, among the ordinary Associations of the faithful which are subject to the Sacred Congregation of the Council. Article III provides ordinaries with a practical and authentic criterion for deciding whether or not it is prudent to approach the Holy See for permission to establish a secular Institute.

In order that any pious Association of the faithful may be erected as a secular Institute in accordance with the Articles which follow, it must have, in addition to the requirements of the common law, the following requisites (§§ 2-4)*: . . .*[2]

This introductory sentence recalls to mind the fact that secular Institutes are generically included among Associations of the faithful, and are subject to their law in all that has not been derogated by the proper norms for this specific type of Association.[3]

The clause *"habeat necesse est requisita"* seems to express requirements which are necessary for validity. Those elements which are required for the valid erection of Associations are likewise necessary for the valid erection of secular Institutes. In the opinion of Larraona[4] this clause is considered to be preceptive only, with

[1] Guay, "Les Instituts séculiers," *RUO,* XVIII (1948), 83*; Larraona, "Comment. in legem peculiarem," *De Institutis Saecularibus,* I, 78.

[2] Ut aliqua pia fidelium Consociatio, ad normam Articulorum qui sequuntur, erectionem in Institutum saeculare consequi valeat, haec (§§ 2-4), praeter alia communia, habeat necesse est requisita: . . . Article III, § 1.

[3] Cf. *supra,* pp. 77-78.

[4] "Comment. in legem peculiarem," *De Institutis Saecularibus,* I, 81-82.

regard to the specific requirements enumerated in the following paragraphs of this Article; if it happened that an Institute which *de facto* did not possess the requirements mentioned in §§ 2-4 were to be erected according to law (a possibility which seems extremely unlikely), the validity of its establishment could not be called into question.

Article I. Profession of the Evangelical Counsels

The particular requirements which distinguish secular Institutes from other secular Associations are set forth in numbers 2-4.

With regard to the consecration of life and the profession of Christian perfection:

Persons who desire to be enrolled in the Institutes as members in the strict sense, in addition to practicing those exercises of devotion and mortification which all must undertake who aspire to a life of Christian perfection, must effectively tend toward that same perfection in the special ways which are here enumerated:

1° *By profession before God of celibacy and perfect chastity, which is made secure by vow, oath, or consecration binding in conscience, according to the Constitutions;*

2° *By a vow or promise of obedience of such a nature that they dedicate themselves entirely to God and to the works of charity or of the apostolate by a firm bond, and in all respects are always morally in the hands and under the guidance of their Superiors, according to the Constitutions;*

3° *By a vow or promise of poverty, in virtue of which they have not the free use of temporal goods, but a defined and limited use, according to the Constitutions.*[5]

---

[5] Quoad vitae consecrationem et christianae perfectionis professionem.

Sodales, qui ut membra strictiore sensu sumpta, Institutis adscribi cupiunt, praeter illa pietatis et abnegationis exercitia, quibus omnes, qui ad perfectionem vitae christianae adspirant, incumbant necesse est, ad ipsam peculiaribus etiam rationibus, quae hic recensentur efficaciter tendere debent:

1° Professione nempe coram Deo facta coelibatus et castitatis perfectae,

In treating of members in the strict sense, the Special Law implies the possibility of an Institute's having members in a wide or less strict sense. This latter class would include those who for some reason are unable to fulfill all the requirements demanded by law for membership. There may be many fervent souls who desire to assist in the work of the apostolate, but who are prevented by family obligations or parental duties from making the complete consecration which is required. Such persons can profit greatly by the direction, supervision, and spiritual privileges which would result from association with a secular Institute.[6] The Constitutions of each Institute should determine whether it is to have such a class of members, what requirements are to be made for their admission, and what are the privileges in which they participate.

Members of an Institute in the wide sense are not to be confused with extern members who do not live a community life. Since the obligation of the common life is not a general requirement, there will be members in the strict sense who live by themselves in the world. The basis of distinction between interns and externs rests on the fact of the observance or non-observance of the common life, whereas the basis of distinction between members in the strict or in the wide sense is the profession of the evangelical counsels.[7]

---

quae voto, iuramento, consecratione in conscientia obliganti, ad normam Constitutionum, firmetur.

2° Obedientiae voto vel promissione, ita ut stabili vinculo ligati totos Deo et caritatis seu apostolatus operibus se dedicent, et in omnibus sub manu et ductu semper moraliter sint Superiorum, ad normam Constitutionum.

3° Paupertatis voto vel promissione, vi cuius bonorum temporalium usum non liberum habeant, sed definitum ac limitatum, ad normam Constitutionum. . . Article III, § 2.

[6] Members in the wide sense remind one of those lay associates who, in earlier days, affiliated themselves with religious Orders and Congregations in order to aid them in their work and to derive from this contact a support in their efforts towards perfection. One adverts in this matter to the Oblates of St. Benedict and the various Third Orders Secular.

[7] Cf. S. C. de Religiosis, instr. *Cum Sanctissimus,* 19 mart. 1948, n. 7, a —*AAS,* XL (1948), 294.

Only those who are bound in a stabilized manner to the Institute and who make a profession of the three evangelical counsels are eligible for membership in the strict sense. Thus, married people or those who have the obligation of supporting their parents cannot become members in the strict sense.

The Constitutions could provide for membership in the wide sense as a necessary preliminary before final acceptance. Those canons which regulate the postulancy, the novitiate, and the period of temporary profession in religious institutes[8] do not apply to secular Institutes; because of the special dangers of solitary life in the world, a long period of probation and a gradual assimilation into the Institute seem especially desirable. The reasons for restricting the probationary period in religious institutes do not have the same urgency in this case; neither the refusal of acceptance nor the transferral to membership in the strict sense need have any effect on the external manner of life[9] led by a member of a secular Institute.

Since Institutes require of their members complete dedication to the life of perfection, the Constitutions must make provisions for such exercises of piety and Christian self-denial as are necessary for all who aspire to this goal. Such exercises are indispensable for those who live in constant contact with the world minus the safeguards of the common life or of the religious habit. The dangers of an intensively active life without contemplation can be avoided only if the Institutes have a profoundly supernatural basis.[10] The doctrinal aspect of canon 593 of the law for religious[11] may well be extended to apply, *mutatis mutandis,* to members of secular Institutes.

---

[8] Cans. 539, 555, 574.

[9] I.e., with regard to occupation, place of dwelling, dress, etc.

[10] Larraona ("Comment. in legem peculiarem," *De Institutis Saecularibus,* I, 87) makes this wise observation: "Illa Instituta approbari nec debent nec possunt quae profunde supernaturalia non sint. Melius sane pauca *optima,* quam satis numerosa sed mediocria."

[11] Omnes et singuli religiosi, Superiores aeque ac subditi, debent, non solum quae nuncuparunt vota fideliter integreque servare, sed etiam secundum regulas et constitutiones propriae religionis vitam componere atque ita ad perfectionem sui status contendere.

In addition to the practice of the ordinary exercises of piety which must be undertaken by all who strive after perfection, members of secular Institutes have the special and particular obligation of binding themselves to the observance of the three evangelical counsels.

In the first place, profession must be made of celibacy and perfect chastity, and confirmed by vow, oath, or consecration binding in conscience, according to the Constitutions. The object of this obligation is twofold: celibacy, which forbids subsequent marriage and the use of marriage already contracted, and perfect chastity, which includes both external and internal acts. The particular means employed in the assuming of this obligation is to be determined by the Constitutions. Either a vow, an oath, or a consecration can be made, and it is noteworthy that the making of a promise is not here mentioned, as it is with regard to the obligations of poverty and of obedience. Many Institutes, desiring to avoid any technical terms which would lead to their being confused with religious institutes prefer the term "consecration", which seems very well suited for giving expression to the complete dedication and surrender made by their members.[12]

Whether such an engagement be made in the form of a vow, of an oath, or of a consecration, the profession of celibacy imposes a new obligation—grave *ex genere suo*—which is based on the virtue of religion. Therefore, any violation of this dedication is a sin against the virtue of religion, as well as against the virtue of chastity.[13] This profession, however, is not public in the strict juridic sense, and does not render sacred those who make it. Consequently, the special malice of sacrilege would not be present in acts which violate this profession.[14]

[12] The consecration here mentioned is not to be confused with the liturgical ceremony of the consecration of virgins, according to the rite described in the Roman Pontifical. This solemn consecration cannot be accorded to virgins living in the world (decr. S. C. de Religiosis, 25 mart. 1927—*AAS,* XIX [1927], 138), and is now reserved to nuns with solemn vows (Pius XII, const. ap. *Sponsa Christi,* 21 nov. 1950, Art. III, § 3—*AAS*, XLIII [1951], 16).

[13] Cf. cans. 1307, § 1, and 1317, §1.

[14] This was explicitly stated in a response of the Sacred Congregation

The obligation of obedience arises from a vow made to God, binding under the virtue of religion, or from a promise made to the Superior, binding under the virtue of fidelity.[15] A member must make a complete holocaust of his own will, so that he is dedicated entirely to God and to the works of charity or of the apostolate. His place of domicile and his job or profession are chosen out of obedience, and are subject to change at the will of his superiors. Even though he lives by himself in the world, he should always feel himself under the eye of his superior, both in matters ascetic and disciplinary and in all that pertains to the apostolate.[16] Concrete norms defining the precise authority of superiors over the life and conduct of their subjects will be given by the Constitutions, which will also specify the gravity of particular violations of the obligation of obedience.

With regard to poverty, a member of a secular Institute is limited in the use of his temporal goods. Even after the vow or promise (or, it seems, promissory oath) of poverty, he retains the right to own and to acquire property, but he no longer has the right to the arbitrary, unlimited use of the goods which he possesses. Therefore those canons which regulate the vow of poverty for religious (e.g. cans. 569; 580, §§ 2 and 3; 583) need not necessarily be applied to all secular Institutes.[17] Once again, the Constitutions, having in mind the special nature, scope, and purpose of the particular Institute, will contain practical and concrete

---

of Religious, dated May 19, 1949. The text of this document, together with a similar declaration and a short commentary, may be found in *De Institutis Saecularibus,* I, 182-188.

[15] Although it is not explicitly mentioned in the Law, it seems that a promissory oath (uniting the obligations of fidelity and of religion) could be taken.

[16] Lemoine, "Commentary," *Secular Institutes,* p. 79.

[17] The difficulty of making general statements which will apply to all Institutes once more becomes evident, since the approved Rule of one Institute (The Society of the Women of Nazareth—known also as the Ladies of the Grail) explicitly applies the provisions of the above listed canons to its members.

regulations which will insure a true and real life of poverty in the world.[18]

In relation to the obligation of poverty, some mention must be made of the extension of canon 142 to members of secular Institutes. This canon, which forbids clerics to conduct business or trade (either personally or through agents, either for their own benefit or for that of other persons), is also binding on religious in virtue of can. 592 (and on members of Societies of the Common Life, in virtue of can. 679), but would not be expected to apply to members of secular Institutes, since as a general rule they have neither the obligations nor the privileges of clerics. However, the recent decree of the Sacred Congregation of the Council,[19] which decreed that a *latae sententiae* excommunication specially reserved to the Holy See would be incurred by those who were guilty of violating the provisions of canon 142, explicitly included members of secular Institutes.[20] Most commentators on this decree, interpreting it according to the proper meaning of the words, simply declare that members of secular Institutes are bound in exactly the same way as clerics and religious.[21]

---

[18] Thus, in practice, a member of an Institute will often draw up a budget, with the approval of the superior, which will enable him to live in decent comfort according to his particular social standing. The rest of his income will be sent to the Institute or given to some approved ecclesiastical or charitable work. For extraordinary expenditures which would exceed this budget, the member would then be required to ask permission in each case. Likewise the Constitutions will determine whether or not a member is allowed (or even urged) to enroll himself in a health or hospitalization plan, to take out insurance or annuities, etc.

[19] *Pluribus ex documentis,* 22 mart. 1950—*AAS,* XLII (1950), 330-331.

[20] The pertinent words of the decree are: "... Sanctissimus Dominus Noster Pius Pp. XII statuere dignatus est ut Clerici et Religiosi omnes ritus latini de quibus in canonibus 487-681, ne exceptis quidem recentium Institutorum saecularium sodalibus . . . mercaturam seu negotiationem cuiusvis generis, etiam argentariam exercentes. . ." (It is rather surprising to find that members of Societies of the Common Life are here referred to, at least implicitly, as *"religiosi"*.)

[21] Cf. Smiddy, "Negotiatio," *The Jurist* (Washington, D. C., 1941—), XI (1951), 940; Delchard, "Commentaire," *NRT,* LXXII (1950), 733-734; Creusen, "Commerce Interdit," *RCR,* XXII (1950), 188; Conway, "Im-

Such an interpretation, however, seems to the present writer to be contrary to the very nature and purpose of secular Institutes. The Holy Father has repeatedly praised and encouraged those who seek perfection while remaining undistinguishable from other persons in the world, and who engage in an apostolate which is forbidden or inaccessible to priests and religious.[22] In recognizing and approving the new secular Institutes, the Holy See has insisted that their *secular* character be preserved and that anything inconsistent with this character be avoided; in the words of Pius XII, "this apostolate of the secular Institutes is to be faithfully practiced not only *in the world,* but, as it were, *of the world,* and therefore with avowed aims, practices, forms, and in places and circumstances corresponding to this secular condition."[23]

To prohibit all profit-seeking business and trade to members of secular Institutes would seriously undermine and perhaps destroy completely the essential and specific purpose for which these new groups have been approved by the Church. It is true that speculation in stocks and bonds does not seem fitting for those who have dedicated themselves to a life of perfection, but it is difficult to see any intrinsic incompatibility between the carrying on of a just and licit business enterprise and the pursuit of perfection. Moreover, it must be recalled that when members of a secular Institute engage in business, there is no possibility of scandal, since their identity as members is not known to those among whom they live and work. In addition, it does not seem equitable to impose an obligation of clerics on those who are denied the privileges of clerics.

For all these reasons, a literal application of canon 142 to mem-

---

portant New Decree on *Negotiatio," IER,* 5. series, LXXIV (1950), 366; "Adnotationes," *ME,* LXXV (1950), 179; McReavy, "Negotiatio Clericis Prohibita," *The Clergy Review* (London, 1931—), XXXVI (July, 1951), 11.

[22] E.g., const. ap. *Provida Mater Ecclesia,* 2 febr. 1947—*AAS,* XXXIX (1947), 117, 118.

[23] Motu propr. *Primo feliciter,* 12 mart. 1948, n. II—*AAS,* XL (1948), 285. This statement is even more forceful when read in its context. Cf. also S. C. de Religiosis, instr. *Cum Sanctissimus,* 19 mart. 1948, n. 7, d—*AAS,* XL (1948), 296.

bers of secular Institutes seems unintelligible. Perhaps the decree merely meant to state emphatically that it is binding on all clerics and religious without exception, i.e., even those clerics and religious[42] who are members of secular Institutes. Or, as Gutiérrez suggests,[25] the decree can be interpreted as intending to bind members when they act collectively or in the name of the Institute, rather than in their individual lives. It might also be understood as applying only to the Institutes themselves, as ecclesiastical moral persons. At any rate, the present writer believes that a strict and literal interpretation of this decree would prove to be gravely detrimental to the work of secular Institutes and is contrary to the mind of the legislator as expressed in all the other laws which the Church has passed in regard to Institutes.

The Special Law contains no explicit provisions for the annulment, commutation, or dispensation of the obligations assumed by members of secular Institutes. Certainly, if an absolute vow of perfect and perpetual chastity has been taken by one who is at least eighteen years old, this private vow is reserved to the Holy See.[26] As in the case of Societies of the Common Life, the Constitutions should state who is competent to relax the obligations induced by the vows or promises of poverty and obedience.[27]

Article II. Incorporation

With regard to the incorporation of members in their own Institute and the bond arising therefrom:

The bond by which the secular Institute and its members in the strict sense are to be united must be:

---

[24] It is possible, by way of exception, for a person to be both a religious and a member of a secular Institute; cf. *supra*, p. 74, note 21, and *infra*, p. 120.

[25] "De vetita clericis et religiosis negotiatione mercatura," *CpRM*, XXX (1951), 152. This canonist, who is a member of the Sacred Congregation of Religious, gives many arguments to support the interpretation stated here.

[26] Can. 1309.

[27] For some interesting observations on this point, cf. Delchard, "Consecration," *RDC*, I (1951), 297-298.

1° *Enduring, in accordance with the Constitutions, either for life or for a set period, in which latter case it must be renewed upon expiration (c. 488, 1°);*

2° *Mutual and complete, so that in accordance with the Constitutions, the member hands himself wholly over to the Institute, and the Institute takes care of and is responsible for the member.*[28]

It has already been stated that the Church gives legal recognition only to the *social* profession of perfection.[29] The necessity of observing the common life in the formal sense implies incorporation into an organized group,[30] and this incorporation gives rise to a bond which unites the Institute and its members to each other.[31] This mutual bond must have that stability which is necessary to constitute a *state* of perfection. It is clear that a vow or a promise which is perpetual insures stability. However, the Special Law,

---

[28] Quoad incorporationem Sodalium Instituto proprio et quoad vinculum ex ipsa ortum.

Vinculum quo Institutum saeculare et ipsius membra, proprie dicta, inter se coniungi oportet, debet esse:

1° Stabile, ad normam Constitutionum, sive perpetuum sive temporarium, elapso tempore renovandum (c. 488, 1°);

2° Mutuum ac plenum, ita ut, ad normam Constitutionum, Sodalis se totum Instiuto tradat, et Institutum de Sodali curam gerat atque respondeat... Article III, § 3.

[29] *Supra*, pp. 72-74.

[30] A word must be said here of a new form of the apostolate which could be easily confused with a secular Institute. There are an ever increasing number of young women who live completely consecrated lives in the world by dedicating all that they are and have to the service of the Church in the particular work assigned to them by their bishop. Although these young women are given a common formation (without being withdrawn from their ordinary occupation) and are subject to common statutes, they do not belong to any organized group. Their vocation, closely paralleling that of a secular priest, is to live the life of perfection in the world in perfect submission to the bishop, without being incorporated into any organization. Because of this lack of incorporation, these young women do not form a secular Institute, despite the fact that they have dedicated themselves to the practice of the evangelical counsels in the world.

[31] This requirement indicates a substantial difference between secular Institutes and other Associations of the faithful, since membership in the latter does not imply any such abiding bond.

referring to canon 488, 1°, also allows a temporary engagement, which is to be renewed after the lapse of a fixed time. Such a temporary vow or promise should be perpetual in the intention of the subject; if he deliberately intended not to renew it, the required stability would be lacking. It is true that a temporary engagement is not final or definitive, since the subject is perfectly free not to renew it when the determined time elapses, but he must originally intend renewal.[32]

Consequently, as Creusen points out,[33] groups of the faithful who would devote themselves to the works of the apostolate for some undetermined time, but without the intention of a perpetual engagement and without renouncing the right to establish a family, cannot aspire to become a secular Institute.

The bond of incorporation must also be mutual and complete: the member gives himself completely to the Institute, and the Institute assumes the care of, and responsibility for, the member. Incorporation into a secular Institute, like religious profession, effects a bilateral contract in a proper, but less strict, sense, inasmuch as the reciprocal obligations to which it gives rise are binding, not in commutative justice, but in legal or distributive justice.[34] Again, it must be understood that these mutual rights and duties of the Institute and its members are to be measured according to the provisions of the particular Constitution.

Article III. Possession of Common Houses

With regard to the common buildings or houses of the Institute:

Even though secular Institutes do not impose upon all their members the obligation of the common life or of living under the

[32] Perhaps this would be clarified in the light of an analogously postulated requirement on the part of a candidate for the priesthood: when such a man receives tonsure or minor orders, he does not bind himself definitively, but he does imply his intention of going on to receive major orders. —Guay, "Les Instituts séculiers," *RUO,* XVIII (1948), 88*.

[33] "Les Instituts séculiers," *RCR,* XX (1948), 171.

[34] Cf. O'Neill, *The Dismissal of Religious in Temporary Vows,* pp. 72-73; Frey, *The Act of Religious Profession,* The Catholic University of America Canon Law Studies, n. 63 (Washington, D. C.: The Catholic University of America, 1931), pp. 5-7.

same roof (Art. II, § 1), nevertheless they should, either for necessity or for convenience, have one or several common houses in which:

1° *Those may dwell who exercise authority in the Institute, especially on the supreme or regional level;*

2° *Members can live or to which they can come in order to receive and complete their training, to take part in spiritual exercises, and for other reasons of a similar kind;*

3° *Members can be received when, because of ill health or for other reasons, they cannot provide for themselves, or when it is not advisable that they live privately, either by themselves or with others.*[35]

After stating the necessity of the common life in the formal sense (i.e., incorporation), the Special Law goes on to treat of the common life in the material sense—an element which is present in Institutes in a very limited degree. The Constitutions of a particular Institute may require all its members to live in common,[36] but, as has already been stated,[37] there is no general regulation imposing this requirement on all Institutes.

---

[35] Quoad communes Institutorum saecularium sedes ac domos.

Instituta saecularia, etsi communem vitam seu commorationem sub eodem tecto cunctis suis membris ad normam iuris non imponant (Art. II, § 1), tamen pro necessitate, vel utilitate unam vel plures communes domos habere oportet, in quibus:

1° Residere valeant qui Instituti regimen, supremum praecipue vel regionale, exercent.

2° Commorari vel ad quas convenire queant Sodales, ad institutionem accipiendam et complendam, ad exercitia spiritualia peragenda et ad alia huiusmodi.

3° Recipi possint Sodales, qui ob infirmam valetudinem, vel ob alia rerum adiuncta sibi providere non valeant, vel quibus non expediat, ut apud se vel apud alios ipsi privatim remaneant... Article III, § 4.

[36] It must be clearly understood that such an Institute does not thereby become a Society of the Common Life, since the common life in the latter is governed by the prescriptions of the Code. This fact is insisted upon repeatedly by Larraona, "Comment. in legem peculiarem," *De Institutis Saecularibus,* I, 60, 61, 96, 97, 100.

[37] *Supra,* pp. 72-74.

Nevertheless, the Special Law does prescribe that every Institute have one or more common houses. From the wording of this Article, the possession of a central house seems necessary before the erection of a diocesan Institute, but the Holy See would grant permission for the foundation of an Institute if it is striving to acquire such a house.[38] The decree of praise will be granted only to an Institute which actually possesses one or more common houses.

The possession of a central house is advisable or necessary for three principal[39] reasons. In the first place, every organized group must have a headquarters of some kind. A central house is necessary for the internal government of a secular Institute, so that the superior and the members can readily communicate with one another; it is also beneficial as a means of facilitating the external relations of the Institute, e.g., with the diocesan authorities. It is fairly obvious that the supreme or regional superiors must have some fixed residence, so that they are easily accessible to all who find it necessary to contact them.

A common house is also desirable as a center for spiritual and intellectual formation. Since members are definitively incorporated into an Institute only after a long period of probation, it would be expedient to provide a meeting-place at which members could gather at regular intervals. In this way a definite program of studies could be offered, and members could make their monthly days of recollection and their annual retreat. An arrangement of this kind would also be instrumental in fostering a desired sense of solidarity and *esprit de corps*.

Finally, an Institute would find it useful to have a place where it could accommodate members who, because of sickness or of old age, could no longer take care of themselves. Such a house could also serve as a temporary haven for those members who, because of some particular circumstances or dangers, consider it unwise to

[38] S. C. de Religiosis, Instr. *Cum Sanctissimus,* 19 mart. 1948, n. 7, c—*AAS,* XL (1948), 296.

[39] It is quite clear that the three reasons given do not constitute an all-inclusive enumeration of the causes which give rise to the necessity of possessing common houses.

continue living alone in the world. The Constitutions determine the exact financial responsibility of a particular Institute to its members. Those which have adopted the provisions of canon 580, § 2, will directly assume the care of members unable to provide for themselves. Institutes which allow members to retain their earnings have a correspondingly limited financial responsibility, but are bound, at least in charity, to see that their members are provided for in some way.

CHAPTER VII

Establishment of Secular Institutes

Article I. Institutes of Diocesan Approval

Section 1. Competent authority

Bishops, but not vicars capitular or vicars general, can establish secular Institutes and confer on them the status of moral persons, in accordance with canon 100, §§ 1 and 2.

Bishops should not, however, establish these Institutes nor should they allow them to be established without consulting the Sacred Congregation of Religious, in accordance with canon 492, § 1, and the Article which here follows.[1]

With regard to their canonical foundation, secular Institutes do not follow the general norms governing Associations of the faithful;[2] the Special Law here adapts and applies to them the prescriptions contained in the Code for the erection of religious Congregations.[3]

In practice a secular Institute is usually founded by a group of the faithful under the guidance of a priest, but its juridic establishment, by which it acquires moral personality, is reserved exclusively to the bishop. The term "bishop," as used here, does not include titular bishops,[4] but does extend to local ordinaries who have the same jurisdiction as residential bishops, even though

---

[1] Instituta saecularia Episcopi, non autem Vicarii Capitulares vel Generales condere et in personam moralem, ad normam c. 100, §§ 1 et 2, erigere possunt.

Ea tamen Instituta Episcopi ne condant neque condi sinant, inconsulta Sacra Congregatione de Religiosis, ad normam c. 492, § 1, et Art., qui sequitur... Article V, §§ 1 and 2.

[2] Associations of the faithful can be established without permission of the Holy See, and can be erected by a vicar general who acts in virtue of a special mandate—can. 686, §§ 2 and 4.

[3] Can. 492, § 1.

[4] Can. 348, § 1.

they do not possess the episcopal character. Thus vicars and prefects apostolic,[5] abbots and prelates *nullius,*[6] and apostolic administrators who are permanently constituted[7] are competent to erect secular Institutes.

Vicars capitular and vicars general are explicitly denied the right of foundation. This prescription has an invalidating effect, so that if either of these attempted to establish an Institute the foundation would be invalid. The bishop, however, has ordinary power in this matter and can delegate this power to his vicar general if he chooses. The vicar general can validly and licitly erect a secular Institute only if he has been explicitly delegated by the bishop. Since no mention is made here of a vicar general acting in virtue of a special mandate, it is clear that in this particular instance the vicar general would not have ordinary power even if he possessed such a special mandate.

The legal establishment of an Institute automatically confers moral personality upon the Institute. In accordance with the prescriptions of canon 100, § 2, an Institute must have at least three members before the bishop can establish it. When the bishop, having obtained permission from the Sacred Congregation of Religious, issues a formal decree of erection, the Institute becomes an ecclesiastical moral person, which is capable of possessing rights and duties, and which is by its nature perpetual.[8]

In order to prevent the useless and imprudent multiplication of new Institutes, bishops[9] are required to consult the Sacred Congregation of Religious[10] before proceeding to erect a new Institute.

---

[5] Can. 294, § 1.

[6] Cans. 215, § 2 and 323, § 1.

[7] Can. 315, § 1.

[8] Can. 102.

[9] The duty of consultation is incumbent upon the bishop, rather than upon the lay founder of the proposed Institute. The Instruction *Cum Sanctissimus,* in n. 3, explicitly states: "To obtain permission to erect a new secular Institute, the bishop of the place, *and no other,* must apply to this Sacred Congregation. . ."—*AAS,* XL (1948), 294 (italics added).

[10] Whereas can. 492, § 1, prescribes consultation with the Holy See (for the erection of religious Congregations), this Article explicitly mentions the Sacred Congregation of Religious. Therefore, in the opinion of the

However it must be admitted that this prescribed consultation is not necessary for the validity of the foundation. Canonical commentators generally agree[11] that, if a bishop issued a decree of erection without having previously consulted the Holy See, the foundation would be made unlawfully but nevertheless validly. In this case the Holy See could later invalidate the foundation, and the offending bishop could be held liable for punishment. Certainly the Holy See would not recognize an Institute erected without its permission until this canonical defect had been corrected.

As Ristuccia remarks,[12] the consultation with the Holy See ought to be more than a mere notification or the simple seeking of advice; it consists rather in a request for the permission of the Holy See . However, when this permission is granted, the Holy See replies in the negative form of a *nihil obstat,* which differs completely from the positive decree of praise or of pontifical approval.

It is of practical importance to note that the bishop is required to consult the Sacred Congregation only when he intends to erect a secular Institute *as such.* A group which hopes to receive approval as a secular Institute will usually begin as a simple Association of the faithful, and will remain in this form under the prudent supervision of the bishop. The Holy See presumes that groups have passed through a successful period of probation be-

---

present writer, vicars and prefects apostolic who desire to establish secular Institutes in missionary countries should apply to the Sacred Congregation of Religious, rather than to the Sacred Congregation for the Propagation of the Faith, unless it be a question of a clerical Institute which is founded exclusively for missionary purposes. Cf. *supra,* pp. 81-82.

[11]E.g., Coronata, *Institutiones,* I, 626, note 3; Vermeersch-Creusen, *Epitome, I,* 447; Beste, *Introductio,* p. 319; Cappello, *Summa Iuris Canonici* (3 vols., Vol. II, 4. ed., Romae: Apud Aedes Universitatis Gregorianae, 1945), II, 11; Schaefer, *De Religiosis,* p. 115; De Carlo, *Ius Religiosorum* p. 18; Pejska, *Ius Canonicum Religiosorum,* p. 15; Orth, *The Approbation of Religious Institutes,* p. 118; Larraona, "Commentarium Codicis," *CpR,* V (1924), 48. These passages refer to religious Congregations, but the argument applies, *a pari,* to secular Institutes.

[12] *Quasi-Religious Societies,* p. 77.

fore they apply for permission to be erected as secular Institutes.[13] Therefore the bishop can and should establish such preliminary groups on his own authority—without consulting the Holy See—, even though it is foreseen that they will later develop into secular Institutes. It is only after the bishop judges that such groups have given sufficient signs of their vitality and have merited approbation as secular Institutes that he will apply to the Sacred Congregation for permission to erect them as such.

Section 2. Prescribed procedure

When bishops, in accordance with Art. V, § 2, consult the Sacred Congregation of Religious in advance for the purpose of securing permission to establish Institutes, this Sacred Congregation, in order to grant such permission, must be informed of all those matters which are specified in the Norms issued by the same Sacred Congregation for the establishment of a Congregation or a Society of the Common Life of diocesan approval (nn. 3-5), due allowances being made for those differences between the respective cases which the Sacred Congregation shall determine; it shall also be informed of other matters which the practice and procedure of the same Sacred Congregation have required or will require in the future.

When the bishops have obtained the permission of the Sacred Congregation of Religious, there will be nothing to prevent them from freely using their right and establishing the Institute. Bishops

---

[13] S. C. de Religiosis, instr. *Cum Sanctissimus,* 19 mart. 1948, nn. 5 and 6—*AAS,* XL (1948), 294-295. In n. 7 of this same Instruction, bishops are provided with practical norms for judging whether or not an association has the essential marks of a secular Institute. The points to be considered are as follows: a) whether the members profess in a practical and substantial way the three evangelical counsels; b) whether the bond between the members and the association is enduring, reciprocal, and complete; c) whether and how the association is striving to acquire the prescribed common houses; d) whether such things are avoided as are inconsistent with the nature and character of secular Institutes, such as a habit unlike the ordinary dress of the world, or a common life that is externally organized in the same way as religious community life.

should not fail to send official notice to the same Sacred Congregation that the establishment has taken place.[14]

In consulting the Sacred Congregation of Religious before establishing a secular Institute, the bishop is required to follow, as far as possible, the procedure prescribed for the foundation of a religious Congregation or of a Society of the Common life of diocesan approval. The matter upon which the Sacred Congregation is to be informed has been clearly detailed by the Holy See.[15] Thus the bishop must not only tell the name of the founder of the new Institute, but must also give an account of his character and of the motives which have led him to desire the founding of the Institute. The report must also indicate the name or title of the new Institute, the number and type of works which it intends to assume, and its means of support. Mention must also be made whether or not there are similar Institutes already existing in the diocese and, if so, what their activities are.[16]

The phrase *congrua congruis referendo* makes it clear that certain requirements which are prescribed for the obtaining of per-

---

[14] Ut Episcopis, de erectione Institutorum ad normam Art. V, § 2 in antecessum consulentibus, Sacra Congregatio de Religiosis licentiam concedat eadem erigendi, de iis, congrua congruis ipsius iudicio referendo, edoceri debet, quae pro erectione Congregationis Societatisve vitae communis iuris dioecesani in Normis ab eadem Sacra Congregatione impertitis definiuntur (nn. 3-5) atque de aliis quae ex stilo et praxi eiusdem Sacrae Congregationis inducta sunt, vel in posterum inducentur.

Obtenta ab Episcopo Sacrae Congregationis de Religiosis licentia, nihil obstabit quomius, ipsi iure proprio uti libere possint et erectionem peragere. De erectione peracta officiale nuntium eidem Sacrae Congregationi Episcopi mittere ne omittant... Article VI, §§ 1 and 2.

[15] *Normae secundum quas Sacra Congregatio de Religiosis in novis religiosis Congregationibus approbandis procedere solet,* 6 mart. 1921—*AAS,* XIII (1921), 312-319 (hereafter cited *Normae* of 1921); S. C. de Religiosis decr. *Quod. iam,* 30 nov. 1922—*AAS,* XIV (1922), 644-646. Cf. also Leo XIII, const. *Conditae a Christo,* 8 dec. 1900—Fontes, n. 644; Beat. Pius X, motu propr. *Dei Providentis,* 16 iul. 1906—*Fontes,* n. 675. (There is no English version of the *Normae* of 1921, for the Holy See has prohibited their translation, but the Latin text can be found in Schaefer, *De Religiosis,* pp. 124-129.

[16] *Normae* of 1921, n. 4—*AAS,* XIII (1921), 313.

mission to erect a religious Congregation are not applicable with reference to the founding of secular Institutes. For example, the *Normae* of 1921[17] require the bishop to report on the form, color, and material of the habit to be worn by the novices and the profesed; obviously, this information is not required in the petition for permission to establish secular Institutes, since their members do not wear a religious habit. It is the prerogative of the Sacred Congregation to judge wherein these differences lie, and to make the necessary adaptations to the regulations governing religious Congregations, so that they become applicable to secular Institutes.

Finally, the bishop must include information which is required by the practice and procedure of the Sacred Congregation. For example, although it is not explicitly prescribed by the *Normae* of 1921, it is now necessary to transmit copies of the Institute's Constitutions, which the Sacred Congregation will read and return to the bishop with pertinent annotations (without, however, giving positive approbation to them).[18]

Once the bishop has received the permission of the Sacred Congregation of Religious, he can proceed to establish the Institute. In doing so, he acts not as a delegate, but in his own name. Strictly speaking, he is not obliged to erect the Institute, even though he has received permission to do so. On the other hand, he cannot establish the Institute unless the particular conditions and pre-

---

[17] *Loc. cit.*

[18] "At least six copies of the Constitutions must be submitted in Latin (or in some other language acceptable to the Curia), together with copies of the Directory and of other documents that may serve to reveal the nature and spirit of the Association. The Constitutions should contain everything that concerns the nature of the Institute, classes of members, the government, the form of consecration (Art. III, § 2), the bond arising from the incorporation of members (Art. III, § 3), common houses (Art. III, § 4), the training of members, and exercises of piety." S. C. de Religiosis, instr. *Cum Sanctissimus,* 19 mart. 1948, n. 3—*AAS,* XL, (1948), 294. This paragraph of the Instruction applies nn. 3-8 of the *Normae* of 1921 to secular Institutes, whereas Art. VI of the Special Law mentions only nn. 3-5. However, nn. 6-8 refer to requirements for obtaining the decree of praise, rather than for obtaining permission for the diocesan establishment.

scriptions imposed by the Sacred Congregation have been fulfilled.[19]

The act of establishment formally consists in a decree of the bishop erecting an Association into that particular type of moral person that is known as a secular Institute. The formal decree of establishment is to be executed in writing[20] and must express the title and purpose of the Institute.[21] Three copies of this decree must be made, one to be kept in the archives of the Institute, the second to be preserved in the diocesan archives, and the third to be sent to Rome with the official notification of the act of establishment.

Once the Institute has been canonically erected, those houses or centers which had previously been founded with the consent of the proper ordinaries[22] become *ipso facto* part of the Institute.[23] Moreover, for the period of ten years following an Institute's establishment, the bishop of the place has the faculties to dispense from the requirement of age, the time of probation, the years of consecration, and other matters which affect offices in the Institute.[24] It is left to the discretion of the ordinary to determine whether such matters as the probation and consecration in the Association which existed previous to the canonical establishment of the Institute are to be taken into account as fulfilling the requirements of the Constitutions.[25]

---

19 Cf. Beat. Pius X, motu propr. *Dei Providentis,* 16 iul. 1906, n. III—*Fontes,* n. 675.

20 However, the absence of a written decree would not invalidate the act of establishment.

21 S. C. de Religiosis, decr. *Quod. iam,* 30 nov. 1922, n. VII—*AAS,* XIV (1922), 645-646; Bouscaren, *Digest,* I, 269. For further observations on the form and content of this document, cf. Orth, *The Approbation of Religious Institutes,* pp. 111-112.

22 In accordance with the provisions of can. 495, § 1.

23 S. C. de Religiosis, instr. *Cum Sanctissimus,* 19 mart. 1948, n. 11, c—*AAS,* XL (1948), 297.

24 *Ibid.,* b—*AAS,* XL (1948), 297.

25 *Ibid.,* a—*AAS,* XL (1948), 297.

Article II. Institutes of Pontifical Approval

Secular Institutes which shall have obtained approval or the decree of praise from the Holy See become pontifical Institutes (cans. 488, 3°; 673, § 2).

In order that secular Institutes of diocesan approval may qualify to obtain a decree of praise or of approbation, generally (due allowances being made by the Sacred Congregation of Religious for the differences between the respective cases) those conditions are required which, according to the Norms (nn. 6 ff.) and according to the practice and procedure of the same Sacred Congregation, have been or may in the future be prescribed and defined for religious Congregations and Societies of the Common Life.

For the first approval, for the further provisional approval (if necessary), and for the definitive approval of these Institutes and their Constitutions, the following procedure is to be followed:

1° *After the case has been prepared in the usual manner and set forth by the recommendation and explanation of at least one consultor, the first discussion of the case shall take place in the Commission of Consultors, under the leadership of His Excellency, the Secretary of the same Sacred Congregation, or of someone taking his place.*

2° *Then the entire matter is to be submitted to the examination and decision of the full Assembly of the Sacred Congregation, with His Eminence, the Cardinal Prefect of the Sacred Congregation, presiding, and in the presence of learned or more experienced consultors who have been summoned for a more careful scrutiny of the case, as necessity or expediency may suggest.*

3° *The decision of the Assembly shall be reported by His Eminence, the Cardinal Prefect, or by His Excellency, the Secretary, to His Holiness in an audience, and shall thus be submitted to his supreme judgment.*[26]

---

[26] Institua saecularia, quae approbationem vel laudis decretum a Sancta Sede consequuta fuerint, iuris pontificii efficiuntur (cc. 488, 3°; 673, § 2).

Ut Instituta saecularia iuris dioecesani laudis vel approbationis decretum consequi valeant, illa generatim, congrua congruis Sacrae Congregationis

Secular Institutes of diocesan approval are formally local, but virtually universal;[27] like religious Congregations and Societies of the Common Life, they can be raised to the status of pontifical approval. When an Institute has proved its success and effectiveness in the work of the apostolate, and its growth seems assured,[28] it can apply to the Holy See for pontifical approval.

There are several stages in the granting of pontifical approval. Usually the decree of praise is given first, together with the temporary approval of the Constitutions. This decree does not indicate approval in the full sense, but it is a sign that the Institute is pleasing to the Holy See and worthy of commendation. As a rule, another period of probation is required before the Holy See grants final and definitive approval, either to the Institute or to its Constitutions.[29]

---

de Religiosis iudicio referendo, requiruntur, quae ex Normis (nn. 6 sqq.) et ex eiusdem Sacrae Congregationis stilo ac praxi, pro Congregationibus et Societatibus vitae communis praescripta et definita sunt, vel in posterum definientur.

Ad horum Institutorum eorumque Constitutionum primam, ulteriorem, si casus ferat, ac definitivam approbationem ita procedatur:

1° Causae, de more paratae et unius saltem Consultoris voto ac dissertatione illustratae, in Consultorum Commissione, sub ductu Excellentissimi eiusdem Sacrae Congregationis Secretarii aliusve ipsius vices gerentis, prima fiet disceptatio.

2° Inde res tota, praeside Emo Sacrae Congregationis Cardinali Praefecto, atque invitatis ad causam diligentius excutiendam, prout necessitas seu utilitas suggerat, peritis seu peritioribus Consultoribus, pleni Sacrae Congregationis Congressus examini ac decisioni subiiciatur.

3° Congressus resolutio ab Emo Cardinali Praefecto vel ab Excmo Secretario, in Audientia Ssmo Domino referenda Ipsiusque Supremo iudicio submittenda erit... Article VII, §§ 1, 2, and 3.

[27] Larraona, "Comment. in legem peculiarem," *De Institutis Saecularibus,* I, 122.

[28] One of the best reasons for asking the approbation of the Holy See is the fact that the Institute has spread to other dioceses.

[29] By way of exception, the approbation of the Institute may be given immediately (without a decree of praise preceding), or the Constitutions may be approved definitively at the same time that approval is given to the Institute itself. Cf. *Normae* of 1921, n. 12—*AAS,* XIII (1921), 314-315; Schaefer, *De Religiosis,* p. 122; Orth, *The Approbation of Religious* Institutes, p. 134.

The receipt of the simple decree of praise is sufficient to establish an Institute as one of pontifical approval.[30] The decree of praise need not come from the Holy Father personally; usually it will be issued by one of the offices through which the Roman Pontiff is wont to transact the affairs of the universal Church,[31] namely, in this particular case, the Sacred Congregation of Religious.

As a general rule, Institutes which desire to obtain the decree of praise must follow the procedure prescribed for religious Congregations and for Societies of the Common Life. The *Normae* of 1921[32] require the transmission of the following documents to the Holy See: 1) a petition for the decree of praise signed by the supreme moderator of the Institute and his assistants or counsellors; 2) testimonial letters from the ordinaries of the dioceses in which the community has a house, each letter being sent secretly to the Holy See;[33] 3) a report (signed by the supreme moderator and his assistants or counsellors) which gives an account of the origin of the community, the name and qualifications of its founder, the personal, disciplinary, material, and economic status of the community, together with information regarding the establishment of the novitiate and the number and the training of novices and postulants—all of which information is to be authenticated and verified by the bishop in whose diocese the principal house is situated; 4) printed copies[34] of the Constitutions, approved by the bishop, which are to be written in Latin, Italian, or French. The

---

[30] Can. 488, 3°, to which reference is made in this Article, defines a religious institute of pontifical approval as one which has received from the Holy See either approval or at least the decree of praise.

[31] Cf. can. 7.

[32] N. 8—*AAS*, XIII (1921), 314.

[33] As Orth points out (*The Approbation of Religious Institutes*, pp. 146-147), secrecy is required so that the bishop may speak his mind freely and may give his opinion as to whether it is opportune for the Holy See to grant the decree of commendation.

[34] At least ten copies are prescribed by the pre-Code *Normae* issued by the Sacred Congregation of Religious on March 24, 1914—*AAS*, VI (1914), 190.

same procedure is to be repeated when the religious Congregation wishes to obtain final and definitive approval.[35]

Although the Norms made for religious Congregations and for Societies of the Common Life are generally binding on secular Institutes, they are not to be followed completely and indiscriminately. Because of the specific differences between Congregations, Societies, and Institutes, some adaptations must be made. Once again it is stated that the Sacred Congregation of Religious has the exclusive right of determining when such modifications are necessary. Additional requirements which have been or will be induced by the practice and procedure of this Sacred Congregation must also be taken into account.

Number 3 of Article VII describes the procedure which is to be followed by the Sacred Congregation of Religious in granting both the preliminary and the final approval to an Institute and to its Constitutions.[36] The information and documents submitted by the Institute are first given to one of the Consultors, who examines them and draws up his recommendation. The case will then be discussed by the Commission of Consultors,[37] with His Excellency, the Most Reverend Secretary of this Sacred Congregation (or his delegate) presiding. The third step is the more complete examination of the case by the full Assembly of the Sacred Congregation.[38]

This Special Congress, over which His Eminence, the Cardinal Prefect of the Sacred Congregation, should preside, is composed of the major officials of the Sacred Congregation and their assis-

---

[35] *Normae* of 1921, nn. 9-10—*AAS,* XIII (1921), 314.

[36] Since these prescriptions apply to members of the Sacred Congregation, they can only be of academic interest to the readers of this dissertation, and consequently it suffices to give here a short summary of the procedure to be employed.

[37] Viz., the Special Commission for secular Institutes, established in a decree of the Sacred Congregation of Religious under date of March 25, 1947—*AAS* XXXIX (1947), 131-132.

[38] This body is not to be confused with the Plenary Congress of Cardinals which must examine petitions for the preliminary approval of religious Congregations and of Societies of the Common Life. Cf. Larraona, "Comment. in legem peculiarem," *De Institutis Saecularibus,* I, 128.

tants, together with the consultors who have been invited to give expert and technical advice.[39] After a thorough discussion of the case, the Congress[40] reaches a decision as to the advisability of giving pontifical approval to the Institute in question, and submits this decision to the Roman Pontiff, either through the Cardinal Prefect or through the Secretary of the Sacred Congregation. If His Holiness sees fit to confirm this decision in favor of approbation,[41] the Institute is granted the decree of praise, or definitive approval, according to the nature of the petition.

---

[39] The consultors who take part in this discussion need not be the same as those who composed the Commission for the preliminary examination, although these latter can be summoned, if it seems useful.

[40] It may be noted that the consultors are present only in an advisory capacity and do not have the right to vote.

[41] Such a confirmation is given *in forma communi;* cf. Maroto, "Annotationes," *CpR,* IX (1928), 294-296.

CHAPTER VIII

Secular Institutes in Their External and Internal Relations

Article I. Subjection to the Local Ordinary

Secular Institutes, besides being subject to their own laws if they have any or if any be subsequently enacted, are subject to the local ordinaries, according to the law which is in effect for non-exempt Congregations and Societies of the Common Life.[1]

In defining the subjection of secular Institutes to the local ordinary, the legislator once again borrows from the law which governs religious Congregations and Societies of the Common Life. The prescriptions of the Code which prevail for these latter groups in this particular matter are hereby extended to secular Institutes.

In order to determine the relationship of a particular Institute to the local ordinary, it is necessary to take into account the particular class to which the Institute in question belongs. Institutes of diocesan approval follow the norms for Congregations (and Societies) of diocesan approval; those of pontifical approval follow the regulations for Congregations (and Societies) of pontifical approval; clerical Institutes or lay Institutes are governed by the respective canons which rule Congregations (and Societies) of these particular categories.

In a general way it can be said that the relationship between secular Institutes and the local ordinary is one of partial subjection and partial autonomy. Thus, an Institute of diocesan approval, if it has not yet received the decree of praise or of approbation from the Holy See, remains fully subject to the local ordinary, even though it has spread into other dioceses.[2] Even the members of

---

[1] Instituta saecularia, praeterquam propriis, si quae adsint vel in posterum ferentur legibus, ad normam iuris pro non exemptis Congregationibus et Societatibus vitae communis vigentis, Ordinariis locorum subiecta sunt... Article VIII.

an Institute of pontifical approval are subject to the jurisdiction of the local ordinary, unless they have obtained from the Holy See the privilege of exemption.[3] On the other hand, pontifical Institutes are granted a certain degree of autonomy, inasmuch as the ordinary is forbidden to make any change in the Constitutions, to inquire into the temporal administration of the Institute (without prejudice to the provisions of canons 533-535), and to interfere in the internal government and discipline, except in certain definite matters if it be a question of a lay Institute.[4]

Since this Article of the Special Law simply applies to secular Institutes, without modification, those canons of the Code which regulate the relationship between Congregations (and Societies) and local ordinaries, it is beyond the scope of the present work to give a complete statement of, or commentary on, the particular matters involved. It is sufficient to state here that the ordinary has the same rights and obligations with regard to Institutes as he has with regard to Congregations (and Societies) of the corresponding category. A more comprehensive account will be found both in the standard canonical commentaries which treat of the Code in general or of the law for religious in particular, and in specific treatments of this question.[5] With regard to such particu-

---

[2] Can. 492, § 2.

[3] Can. 500, § 1.

[4] Can. 618, § 2, 1°, 2°.

[5] Cf. Gutiérrez, "De gradibus libertatis et subiectionis religiosorum respectu ordinarii loci," *CpRM,* XXII (1941), 28-37, 83-92, 133-143, 213-227, 305-313; XXIII (1942), 30-41, 113-124, 292-298; Fogliasso, *Introductio in vigentem disciplinam de iuridicis relationibus inter religiones et ordinarium loci* (Augustae Taurinorum: Schola Typographica Salesiana, 1948); Freriks, *Religious Congregations in Their External Relations,* The Catholic University of America Canon Law Studies, n. 1 (Washington, D. C.: The Catholic University of America, 1916) (It must be noted that this work appeared before the promulgation of the Code); Quinn, *Relation of the Local Ordinary to Religious of Diocesan Approval,* The Catholic University of America Canon Law Studies, n. 283 (Washington, D. C.: The Catholic University of America Press, 1949); Farrell, *The Rights and Duties of the Local Ordinary Regarding Congregations of Women Religious of Pontifical Approval;* Ristuccia, *Quasi-Religious Societies,* especially pp. 105-110, 172-179; Gallik, *The Rights and Duties of Bishops Regarding*

lar matters as the quinquennial visitation, the election of superiors, the administration and alienation of temporal goods, the financial report, the investment of special gifts, and the supervision of pious bequests, trusts, and foundations, the reader is referred to special studies which consider these questions in detail.[6]

Although this Article applies to secular Institutes the norms for non-exempt Congregations (and Societies), it must not be inferred that Institutes will never be granted the privilege of exemption. As a general rule, Institutes, like Congregations,[7] are not exempt from the jurisdiction of the local ordinary, but it is quite possible that the Holy See may in the future grant the privilege of exemption to some Institute. In this eventuality the scope of exemption will be determined by the words of the document which grants this privilege.

Diocesan Sisterhoods (St. Paul, Minnesota: Wanderer Publishing Co., 1939); Muzzarelli, *Tractatus Canonicus de Congregationibus Iuris Diocesani* (Romae: Apud Piam Societatem a S. Paulo Apostolo, 1943), pp. 52-187.

[6] E.g., Reilly, *The Visitation of Religious,* The Catholic University of America Canon Law Studies, n. 112 (Washington, D. C.: The Catholic University of America, 1938), pp. 84-115; Parsons, Canonical Elections, The Catholic University of America Canon Law Studies, n. 118 (Washington, D. C.: The Catholic University of America Press, 1939), pp. 134-137, 154-155, 182-185, 210-212; McManus, *The Administration of Temporal Goods in Religious Institutes,* The Catholic University of America Canon Law Studies, n. 109 (Washington, D. C.: The Catholic University of America, 1937), pp. 55-164; Heston, *The Alientation of Church Property in the United States,* The Catholic University of America Canon Law Studies, n. 132 (Washington, D. C.: The Catholic University of America Press, 1941), pp. 114-116, 151-188; Comyns, *Papal and Episcopal Administration of Church Property,* The Catholic University of America Canon Law Studies, n. 147 (Washington, D. C.: The Catholic University of America Press, 1942), pp. 68-109; Lynch, *Contracts between Bishops and Religious Congregations,* The Catholic University of America Canon Law Studies, n. 239 (Washington, D. C.: The Catholic University of America Press, 1946), pp. 73-194; Hannan, *The Canon Law of Wills,* The Catholic University of America Canon Law Studies, n. 86 (Washington, D. C.: The Catholic University of America, 1934), pp. 451-472.

[7] Can. 618, § 1.

Article II. Internal Government

The internal government of secular Institutes can be organized hierarchically after the manner of the government of religious institutes and Societies of the Common Life, due allowances being made (according to the judgment of the same Sacred Congregation) for the differences between the respective cases, and due account being taken of the nature, the purpose, and the circumstances of the Institutes themselves.[8]

Article VIII states that its is permissible for secular Institutes to imitate the internal organization which prevails in religious institutes and Societies of the Common Life. In allowing Institutes to adopt a hierarchical form of government, the Holy See clearly distinguishes them from ordinary associations of the faithful. These latter Associations can only be local in character, and remain entirely subject to the local ordinary; they cannot be linked with other similar Associations (either outside the diocese or even within the same diocese) by any internal bond of government. Even an archsodality, an archconfraternity, or a primary union which has acquired by indult[9] the right to affiliate with itself other Associations which have the same right and purpose acquires no right over the affiliated group.[10] Likewise sodalities of Third Orders Secular cannot unite in such a way that one group is dependent upon another.[11]

Because of their character as states of perfection, secular Institues differ profoundly from other Associations of the faithful. They can constitute organic bodies with a true internal hierarchy of gov-

---

[8] Regimen internum Institutorum saecularium hierarchice ad instar regiminis Religionum et Societatum vitae communis, congrua congruis eiusdem Sacrae Congregationis iudicio referendo, pro ipsorum Institutorum natura, finibus, et adiunctis ordinari potest. . . Article IX.

[9] Can. 721.

[10] Can. 772, § 2. For a recent example of such an indult, cf. S. C. de Prop. Fide, decr. *De concilio generali Operis Apostolici in Hibernia Constituendo,* 18 nov. 1947—AAS, XL (1948), 423-425; Bousearen, *Digest,* Supplement, pp. 99-101.

[11] Larraona, "Comment. in legem peculiarem," *De Institutis Saecularibus,* I, 135.

ernment; they can be organized on a diocesan, an inter-diocesan, or a universal level.

It is important to note that Articles VIII, unlike the other Articles of the Special Law, is permissive, rather than preceptive. Secular Institutes are not obliged to adopt the form of government followed by religious institutes. Far from imposing uniform, ironclad regulations in this matter, the Holy See manifests great prudence and liberality in allowing such latitude in the choice of a form of government.

Founders of secular Institutes are free to select any of the forms of organization for religious institutes which are recognized in history and accepted by law. It is noteworthy that the generic term *religiones* is here used; consequently, Institutes are permitted to model their internal government after that of Orders, as well as that of Congregations. For the sake of summary, the forms of organization which Institutes may adopt can be reduced to four:

1) Institutes can have a centralized, hierarchical government, similar to that which is found in many Orders and Congregations. This form of organizations has three subordinated levels of authority: the supreme, the provincial, and the local. The supreme moderator, or superior general, has power over all the provinces, houses, and members of the institute.[12] The provinces are composed of several houses which are subject to the provincial superior, who is a major superior with ordinary power.[13] Since the houses of such institutes are not autonomous, they are ruled by the local (minor) superior in complete subjection to the supreme and provincial superiors.

2) Institutes are permitted to organize according to the form which is called by the Code[14] a monastic congregation, i.e., a union of several independent houses under one superior. This is a non-centralized form, which retains some degree of subordination. The Abbot Primate, or superior of the monastic congregation, is a major superior (and, in some cases, the supreme superior), but he does not have the power and jurisdiction which the common law

[12] Can. 502.

[13] Can. 488, 6° and 8°.

[14] Can. 488, 2°.

gives to major superiors; his power and jurisdiction are to be determined by the proper Constitutions and the particular decrees of the Holy See.[15] There are no provinces in the strict juridical sense; each house is autonomous, and the local superior is a major superior.[16]

3) A non-centralized, non-hierarchical form of government is also allowed. Although similar to a monastic congregation, this form insures the complete independence of each house which is governed by a major superior. The autonomous houses are united by a fraternal and moral bond into a federation, but are in no sense subject to this federation, which is a mere collective person, rather than a collegiate person in the strict sense.[17]

4) Finally, Institutes can remain merely local and diocesan in character, if this form corresponds more perfectly to their particular nature and circumstances.

Once again the phrase *congrua congruis referendo* appears as a reminder that the forms of government utilized by religious institutes are not to be copied slavishly by secular Institutes. The Sacred Congregation of Religious has the right of determining what modifications are to be made in order to preserve the essential character of secular Institutes. The choice of a particular form of government should be the result of a consideration both of the generic secular nature of all Institutes and of the particular purpose and conditions of the Institute in question.[18]

---

[15] Can. 501, § 3.

[16] Can. 488, 8°.

[17] Schaefer, *De Religiosis,* pp. 87-88; Larraona, "Comment. in legem peculiarem," *De Institutis Saecularibus,* I, 135-140.

[18] This criterion was restated and enlarged upon by the Holy Father in his motu proprio *Primo feliciter* (n. IV): "A hierarchical interdiocesan and universal organization, after the manner of an organic body, is applicable to secular Institutes (Art. IX), and such application should undoubtedly give them internal vitality, a wider and more effective influence and stability. Yet in this organization, which should be adapted to each particular Institute, the nature of the purpose which the Institute seeks to attain, its possibility of greater or lesser expansion, its degree of development and maturity, its circumstances, and other such matters must all be taken into consideration. Nor should those forms of Institutes be rejected or despised which exist as federations and which wish to retain

It seems appropriate to remark here that the Holy See does not wish secular Institutes to be overdependent upon religious Orders and Congregations. Certainly members of secular institutes are allowed to receive spiritual and moral direction from religious. However, aggregation of a secular Institute to a religious institute[19] requires the obtaining of a special concession from the Sacred Congregation. Permission for a more strict form of dependence, which may detract from the autonomy of government which secular Institutes should have, will not easily be granted.[20]

These regulations are a clear indication of the Church's desire to guard against the danger of an Institute's being transformed into a religious community, since such a transformation would only distort and deform the specific nature of secular Institutes. It can be said that the greater the measure in which Institutes approximate religious organizations, the less effective they will be in their

---

and to promote, with moderation, the local character of a partciular nation, region, or diocese, provided that such character be good and in accord with the catholicity of the Church."—*AAS,* XL (1948), 285.

[19] It must be noted that the prohibition of canon 703, § 1, does not apply here; a Congregation, as well as an Order, can be given the privilege of affiliating with itself a secular Institute.

[20] ". . .a) Although the provisions of canon 500, § 3, do not strictly concern secular Institutes and need not be applied to them as they stand, yet it is possible to draw from them a solid criterion and clear direction for the approval and organizing of secular Institutes.

b) Although according to law (can. 492, § 1) there is nothing to prevent secular Institutes from being aggregated by special concession to Orders and even to other religious institutes and from being helped by these latter in various ways and even in some way being morally directed by them, nevertheless other forms of closer dependence, if they would seem to detract from the autonomy of government of secular Institutes or to subject that autonomy to a more or less stringent control, can be granted only with difficulty, even when such dependence is desired and sought by the Institutes themselves, especially if they be Institutes of women; permission can be granted only with appropriate precautions, after a careful consideration of the welfare of the Institutes and upon deliberation on their spirit and on the nature and character of the apostolate to which they are dedicated."—S. C. de Religiosis, instr. *Cum Sanctissimus,* 19 mart. 1948, n. 9 (*AAS,* XL [1948], 296).

particular and providential apostolate.[21] The repeated insistence of the Holy See that the secular character of Institutes be preserved[22] is rigidly observed by many Institutes, which often go to great lengths to avoid anything that might lead to their being confused with religious institutes.[23]

It is both interesting and indicative to note in the Constitutions of secular Institutes the use of new terms which have been employed in order to emphasize their secular status. In the Constitutions of various Institutes the following terms are found: for "novice," the word "aspirant" is used; for "novitiate," "probation," "formation," or "training"; for "novice master," "spiritual leader," or "counselor"; for "profession," "incorporation," "engagement," "donation," or "dedication"; for "province," "region," "section," or "district"; for "religious house," "center," or "cenacle"; for "supreme moderator," "president general"; for "superior," "rector" or "regent"; for "provincial superior," "regional president" or "regional director"; for "local superior," "director," "house president," or "secretary." In adopting such a new terminology these Institutes are carrying out the very evident intention of the Holy See to avoid whatever might create the false impression that secular Institutes are no different from religious institutes.

---

[21] Larraona, "Comment. in legem peculiarem," *De Institutis Saecularibus,* I, 165; cf. Jombart, "Un Nouvel Etat de Perfection, Les Instituts Séculiers," *RAM,* XXIV (1948), 280-281.

[22] Cf. *supra,* pp. 62, 65-66, and 91.

[23] E.g., it is rather ironic that the very Institute which bears the name *Opus Dei* forbids its lay members to say the Divine Office, on the ground that the recitation of the Office is a devotion pertaining to religious and clerics.

CHAPTER IX

Effect of This Apostolic Constitution

This Apostolic Constitution makes no change with regard to the rights and obligations of Institutes which are already established and which have been approved either by the bishops, after consultation with the Holy See, or by the Holy See itself.[1]

At the time of the promulgation of this Special Law there were in existence societies which possessed the essential characteristics of secular Institutes. Before 1947 the juridic standing of such societies was not clearly defined.[2] Inasmuch as they lacked some of the legally postulated elements of religious institutes,[3] the common law for religious was not entirely applicable to them, and their approbation was largely the result of dispensations and privileges. When the Holy See decided to issue uniform regulations for this new type of society and to define its unique status before the law, it had no intention of infringing on the acquired rights of societies which were already in existence.[4]

This Apostolic Constitution in no way alters the rights and obligations of societies which were approved before 1947, provided that they had been established with at least the negative intervention of the Holy See. Societies which had been erected by bishops after consultation with the Holy See, as well as those which had been directly approved by the Holy See are permitted to retain the rights and obligations which they had prior to the publication of the *Provida Mater Ecclesia.* This special consideration is not

[1] Quoad iura et obligationes Institutorum, quae condita iam sunt et ab Episcopis, consulta Sancta Sede, vel ab ipsa Sancta Sede fuerunt approbata, hac Constitutione Apostolica nihil immutatur... Article X.

[2] Cf. *supra*, pp. 49-50.

[3] E.g., the obligations of living in common and of wearing a religious habit.

[4] Cf. can. 10: Leges respiciunt futura, non praeterita, nisi nominatim in eis de praeteritis caveatur.

extended to societies which existed only *de facto* (rather than *de iure*) at the time at which the Special Law appeared. Likewise Article X does not apply to societies which were legitimately approved by the bishop, without any intervention of the Holy See, as Associations of the faithful. In both of these latter cases there is present what is known in canonical terminology as a *res adhuc integra,* and all the provisions of this Special Law must be followed.

It should be noted that the particular form under which an already existing society had been approved is of no consequence. Before 1947 some groups which possessed the essential and discriminative requirements of secular Institutes had been approved as secular Associations,[5] and others, as Societies of the Common Life,[6] and still others, as religious Congregations.[7] It likewise makes no difference from which Roman Congregation these societies had received approval.[8] In all of the above mentioned instances, the rights and obligations of the society are in no way affected by this Apostolic Constitution.

Article X explicitly states that the non-retroactivity of this Special Law applies only to the *rights* and *obligations* of existing, approved societies. To treat such societies as completely new and to require that they once again be canonically erected would seem to be inequitable. However, by the official recognition of secular Institutes the juridic nature of such societies is completely changed. If a society possesses completely the essential characteristics of this newly-recognized form and lacks some of the elements which the law requires for religious institutes and Societies of the Common Life,[9] it is certainly fitting that it be included among secular Institutes rather than remain as an exception among Congregations and Societies.[10]

---

[5] E.g., the Missionaries of the Kingship of Christ.

[6] E.g., the Institute known as *Opus Dei.*

[7] E.g., the Company of St. Paul.

[8] E.g., the Missionaries of the Kingship of Christ had received the approbation of the Sacred Congregation of the Council.

[9] E.g., the obligation of living the canonical common life.

[10] That already approved societies have an obligation to assume the

In assuming the form of a secular Institute, an existing association will be permitted to retain its particular characteristics, provided that they are compatible, even by way of exception, with the nature of secular Institutes. For example, if the previously approved Constitutions of the society permitted its members to take public vows, this provision may be retained after the society has become a secular Institute, since Institutes can, in exceptional cases, call for public vows from their members.[11] In this way it is possible for a society to be at once a secular Institute and a true religious Congregation. An association which had been approved as a Congregation or as a Society before 1947 does not automatically lose its status by being transformed into a secular Institute; in practice, however, such societies are often quite willing to renounce all ties with a classification to which they never completely belonged, and to adopt the new form which corresponds more perfectly to their nature and purpose.[12]

This Apostolic Constitution also affects existing and approved societies in the matter of competence. All societies which have the nature and characteristics described in this Apostolic Constitution are now subject to the Sacred Congregation of Religious, whether they were established before or after its promulgation.[13] This includes even those societies which had originally been approved by one of the other Sacred Congregations.

In order to clarify and summarize what has been said, it may be helpful to list all the possibilities which can arise, and to indicate the proper procedure in each case. In all the following instances it is presupposed that the societies mentioned possess completely the elements postulated by the Special Law as essential to secular Institutes.

1) Institutes established after 1947 are completely subject to all the provisions of the Special Law.

2) Societies which existed *de facto* but not *de iure* before the

---

form of secular Institutes is clearly stated in the Motu Proprio *Primo feliciter*, nn. I and V—*AAS*, XL (1948), 284 and 286; cf. *supra*, p. 67.

[11] Cf. Article II, § 1, 1°, and *supra*, p. 74, note 21.

[12] This was the case with the Company of St. Paul and the *Opus Dei*.

[13] Cf. *supra*, p. 82.

promulgation of the *Provida Mater Ecclesia* are considered not to have had any legal existence, and accordingly must comply with all the requirements of the new law.

3) Associations which had been approved by the bishop in virtue of canon 686, § 2 (i.e., apart from any consultation with the Holy See), can, if they have sufficiently proved themselves, apply to the Holy See for permission to be erected as diocesan Institutes. In this case, the bishop must be guided by the directions contained in Articles V and VI of the Special Law, and in nn. 2, 3, 5, 6, and 7 of the Instruction *Cum Sanctissimus*.

4) If a society has been erected by the bishop after consultation with the Holy See, it should apply to the Sacred Congregation of Religious for recognition as a secular Institute of diocesan approval.

5) If a society has already received from the Holy See the decree of praise, it should petition the Sacred Congregation of Religious for recognition as a secular Institute of pontifical approval.[14]

6) Even a group which had already been definitively approved by the Holy See (either as a Congregation, or as a Society, or as a secular Association) should be reduced to the form of a secular Institute, and thus take its place in the newly-erected category to which it properly belongs.

---

[14] N. 4 of the Instruction *Cum Sanctissimus* states: "Associations which, prior to the Constitution *Provida Mater Ecclesia,* had been legitimately erected or approved by bishops in accordance with the then existing law, or which had obtained some sort of pontifical approval as associations of lay persons, must send the following documents to this Sacred Congregation in order to obtain recognition from the Sacred Congregation as secular Institutes either of diocesan or of pontifical approval: the documents of erection or approval, the Constitutions under which they have hitherto been governed, a brief account of their history, discipline, and apostolate, and, especially if they be of only diocesan approval, testimonials from bishops in whose dioceses they have houses. After all these have been considered and carefully examined according to the provisions of Articles VI and VII of the Constitution *Provida Mater Ecclesia,* the permission for erection, or the decree of praise, as the case may be, can be granted." —*AAS,* XL (1948), 294.

CONCLUSIONS

1) For a long period in history, only those who took public vows and lived in community were included in the juridic state of perfection. After many centuries, the Church gave similar recognition to those who took simple vows and lived the common life. A further mitigation extended recognition to those who lived in common without any public vows. Finally, the Apostolic Constitution *Provida Mater Ecclesia* has explicitly included among the approved states of perfection secular Institutes, whose members are not required either to live in common or to take any (public) vows (pp. 18-50).

2) Although individual members of secular Institutes have a right to keep their identity secret, it is in keeping with the mind of the Holy See that some publicity be given to the fact that such Institutes exist in the Church (pp. 51-53).

3) The distinctive and unique nature of Institutes lies in their secular character, which is also the whole reason for their existence (pp. 61-62; 65-66; 91; 101, note 13; 115; 117).

4) Since secular Institutes can be either clerical or lay, it is inaccurate and misleading to refer to them generically as "lay institutes" (pp. 63-64).

5) The Special Law for secular Institutes must be said to prevail whenever it conflicts with the provisions of the Code; on the other hand, a future general law regarding Associations of the faithful will not derogate from the Special Law, unless it explicitly states such a derogation (pp. 68-69).

6) The lack of the three public vows of religion distinguishes secular Institutes from religious institutes (pp. 70-72); the absence of the common life (in the material sense) distinguishes them from Societies of the Common Life (pp. 72-74); the complete and total consecration which is required of their members distinguishes them from Third Orders Secular and other Associations of the faithful (pp. 62; 85-94; 113-114).

7) The vows which may be taken in secular Institutes, although

juridically private, are more aptly termed semi-public or social vows (pp. 71-72).

8) It is certain that secular Institutes are included among the legally recognized states of perfection, but, in the opinion of the writer, they do not belong to the complete, public, canonical state of perfection (pp. 80-81).

9) The Sacred Congregation of Religious has exclusive, universal competence over secular Institutes even in countries which are subject to the Sacred Congregation for the Propagation of the Faith, the only exception being the one that receives mention in canon 252, § 3 (pp. 81-82; 99, note 10; 120).

10) It is the opinion of the writer that the prohibitions enacted in canon 142 (regarding the carrying on of business and trade) do not apply to members of secular Institutes in the same way as they do to clerics and religious (pp. 90-92).

11) The consultation with the Sacred Congregation of Religious which is prescribed before a bishop erect a secular Institute cannot be said to be necessary for the validity of the foundation (p. 100).

12) The relationship between secular Institutes and the local ordinary varies according to the different types of Institutes, i.e., in line with whether they be of pontifical or of diocesan approval, clerical or lay, etc. (pp. 110-112).

13) Lest Institutes lose their specific and essential secular character, they are not to be overly dependent upon religious institutes (pp. 116-117).

14) This Apostolic Constitution is not retroactive with regard to the rights and obligations of Institutes which already have been approved, but it does affect them with retroactive force in other matters (pp. 118-121).

APPENDIX

The Special Law for Secular Institutes [1]

Article I

Societies, whether clerical or lay, whose members profess the evangelical counsels in the world, in order to attain Christian perfection and to exercise a full apostolate, come under the special name of Institutes, or secular Institutes; thus are they properly distinguished from other common Associations of the faithful (Part Three, Book II of the Code of Canon Law). Such secular Institutes are subject to the norms of this Apostolic Constitution.

Article II

§ 1. Secular Institutes do not admit the three public vows of religion (cans. 1308, § 1 and 488, 1°), nor do they impose upon all their members the obligation of the common life or of a common domicile, according to the canons (cans. 487 ff. and 673 ff.). Therefore:

1° By law, according to rule, secular Institutes are not religious institutes (cans. 487 and 488, 1°) or Societies of the Common Life (can. 673, § 1), nor can they properly be called such.

2° They are not bound by the proper and special law of religious institutes or Societies of the Common Life, nor can they invoke such law, except when some provision thereof (especially of the law governing Societies without public vows) may by way of exception have been legitimately adapted and applied to them.

§ 2. Institutes, while observing the common norms of canon law which concern them, are governed by the following prescriptions as their proper law, corresponding more closely to their specific character and condition:

1° By the general norms of this Apostolic Constitution, which constitute as it were the special statute of all secular Institutes;

2° By the norms which the Sacred Congregation of Religious may decide to issue, according as necessity demands or experience suggests, by way either of interpreting this Apostolic Constitution or of elaborating and applying it to all or some of these Institutes;

3° By the particular Constitutions, approved according to the following Articles (Arts. V-VIII), which may prudently modify the general rules

[1] The English version given here is the work of the present writer; the Latin text can be found in *AAS,* XXXIX (1947), 120-124. Other official documents on secular Institutes are: the Motu Proprio *Primo feliciter* (*AAS,* XL [1948], 283-286), and the Instruction of the Sacred Congregation of Religious entitled *Cum Sanctissimus* (AAS, XL [1948], 293-297).

of law and the special norms set forth above (nn. 1 and 2) in accordance with the widely differing aims, needs, and circumstances of particular Institutes.

Article III

§ 1. In order that any pious Association of the faithful may be erected as a secular Institute in accordance with the Articles which follow, it must have, in addition to the requirements of the common law, the following requisites (§§ 2-4):

§ 2. With regard to the consecration of life and the profession of Christian perfection:

Persons who desire to be enrolled in the Institutes as members in the strict sense, in addition to practicing those exercises of devotion and mortification which all must undertake who aspire to a life of Christian perfection, must effectively tend toward that same perfection in the special ways which are here enumerated:

1° By profession before God of celibacy and perfect chastity, which is made secure by vow, oath, or consecration binding in conscience, according to the Constitutions;

2° By a vow or promise of obedience of such a nature that they dedicate themselves entirely to God and to the works of charity or of the apostolate by a firm bond, and in all respects are always morally in the hands and under the guidance of their Superiors, according to the Constitutions;

3° By a vow or promise of poverty, in virtue of which they have not the free use of temporal goods, but a defined and limited use, according to the Constitutions.

§ 3. With regard to the incorporation of members in their own Institute and the bond arising therefrom:

The bond by which the secular Institute and its members in the strict sense are to be united must be:

1° Enduring, in accordance with the Constitutions, either for life or for a set period, in which latter case it must be renewed upon expiration (can. 488, 1°);

2° Mutual and complete, so that in accordance with the Constitutions, the member hands himself wholly over to the Institute, and the Institute takes care of and is responsible for the member.

§ 4. With regard to the common buildings or houses of the Institute:

Even though secular Institutes do not impose upon all their members the obligation of the common life or of living under the same roof (Art. II, § 1), nevertheless they should, either for necessity or for convenience, have one or several common houses in which:

1° Those may dwell who exercise authority in the Institute, especially on the supreme or regional level;

2° Members can live or to which they can come in order to receive and complete their training, to take part in spiritual exercises, and for other reasons of a similar kind;

3° Members can be received when, because of ill health or for other reasons, they cannot provide for themselves, or when it is not advisable that they live privately, either by themselves or with others.

Article IV

§ 1. Secular Institutes (Art. I) are subject to the Sacred Congregation of Religious, without prejudice to the rights of the Sacred Congregation for the Propagation of the Faith as set down in canon 252, § 3, with reference to Societies and Seminaries destined to serve the foreign missions.

§ 2. Associations which neither have the nature nor fully profess the purpose described in Article I, and those also which lack any of the elements mentioned in Articles I and III of this Apostolic Constitution, are governed by the law of Associations of the faithful (cans. 684 ff.), and come under the Sacred Congregation of the Council, with a full application however of the prescriptions contained in canon 252, § 3, with reference to the territory of the missions.

Article V

§ 1. Bishops, but not vicars capitular or vicars general, can establish secular Institutes and confer on them the status of moral persons, in accordance with canon 100, §§ 1 and 2.

§ 2. Bishops should not however establish these Institutes nor should they allow them to be established without consulting the Sacred Congregation of Religious, in accordance with canon 492, § 1 and the Article which here follows.

Article VI

§ 1. When bishops, in accordance with Art. V, § 2, consult the Sacred Congregation of Religious in advance for the purpose of securing permission to establish Institutes, this Sacred Congregation, in order to grant such permission, must be informed of all those matters which are specified in the Norms issued by the same Sacred Congregation for the establishment of a Congregation or of a Society of the Common Life of diocesan approval (nn. 3-5), due allowance being made for those differences between the respective cases which the Sacred Congregaetion shall determine; it shall also be informed of other matters which the practice and procedure of the same Sacred Congregation have required or will require in the future.

§ 2. When the bishops have obtained the permission of the Sacred Congregation of Religious, there will be nothing to prevent them from freely using their right and establishing the Institute. Bishops should not fail to send official notice to the same Sacred Congregation that the establishment has taken place.

Article VII

§ 1. Secular Institutes which shall have obtained approval or the decree of praise from the Holy See become pontifical Institutes (cans. 488, 3°; 673, § 2).

§ 2. In order that secular Institutes of diocesan approval may qualify to obtain a decree of praise or of approbation, generally (due allowances being made by the Sacred Congregation of Religious for the differences between the respective cases), those conditions are required which, according to the Norms (nn. 6 ff.) and according to the practice and procedure of the same Sacred Congregation, have been or may in the future be prescribed and defined for religious Congregations and Societies of the Common Life.

§ 3. For the first approval, for the further provisional approval (if necessary), and for the definitive approval of these Institutes and their Constitutions, the following procedure is to be followed:

1° After the case has been prepared in the usual manner and set forth by the recommendation and explanation of at least one consultor, the first discussion of the case shall take place in the Commission of Consultors, under the leadership of His Excellency, the Secretary of the same Sacred Congregation, or of someone taking his place.

2° Then the entire matter is to be submitted to the examination and decision of the full Assembly of the Sacred Congregation, with His Eminence, the Cardinal Prefect of the Sacred Congregation, presiding, and in the presence of learned or more experienced consultors who have been summoned for a more careful scrutiny of the case, as necessity or expediency may suggest.

3° The decision of the Assembly shall be reported by His Eminence, the Cardinal Prefect, or His Excellency, the Secretary, to His Holiness in an audience, and shall thus be submitted to his supreme judgment.

Article VIII

Secular Institutes, besides being subject to their own laws if they have any or if any be subsequently enacted, are subject to the local ordinaries, according to the law which is in effect for non-exempt Congregations and Societies of the Common Life.

Article IX

The internal government of secular Institutes can be organized hierarchically after the manner of the government of religious Institutes and Societies of the Common Life, due allowances being made (according to the judgment of the same Sacred Congregation) for the differences between the respective cases, and due account being taken of the nature, the purpose, and the circumstances of the Institutes themselves.

Article X

This Apostolic Constitution makes no change with regard to the rights and obligations of Institutes which are already established and which have been approved either by the bishops, after consultation with the Holy See, or by the Holy See itself.

BIBLIOGRAPHY

Sources

Acta Apostolicae Sedis, Commentarium Officiale, Romae, 1909-1929; Civitate Vaticana, 1929—.

Acta Sanctae Sedis, 41 vols., Romae, 1865-1908.

Baronius, Caesare, *Annales Ecclesiastici,* ed. A. Theiner, 37 vol.s, Vols. I-XXVIII, Barri-Ducis, 1864-1875; Vols. XXIX-XXXVII, Parisiis, 1876-1883.

Bouscaren, T. Lincoln, *The Canon Law Digest,* 2 vols. and Supplement through 1948, Milwaukee: The Bruce Publishing Co., 1934, 1943, 1949.

Bruns, Hermann, *Canones Apostolorum et Conciliorum Saeculorum IV-VII,* 2 vols., Barolini, 1839.

Bullarii Romani Continuatio Summorum Pontificum, 19 vols., Prati, 1835-1858.

Bullarum Diplomatum et Privilegiorum Sanctorum Romanorum Pontificum Taurinensis Editio, 24 vols. et appendix, Augustae Taurinorum, 1857-1872.

Canones et Decreta Sacrosancti Oecumenici Concilii Tridentini, Editio Novissima ad Fidem Optimorum Exemplarium castigate Impressa (XIX reimpressio stereotypa), Taurini: Marietti, 1913.

Codex Iuris Canonici Pii X Pontificis Maximi iussu digestus, Benedicti Papae XV auctoritate promulgatus, Romae: Typis Polyglottis Vaticanis, 1917.

Codex Regularium Monasticarum et Canonicarum, 6 vols., ed. L. Holstenius; ed. altera, cura M. Brockie, Augustae Vindelicorum, 1759.

Codicis Iuris Canonici Fontes, cura Emi Petri Card. Gasparri editi, 9 vols., Romae (postea Civitate Vaticana): Typis Polyglottis Vaticanis, 1923-1939. (Vols. VII-IX, ed. cura et studio Emi Iustiniani Card. Serédi).

Collectanea in Usum Secretariae Congregationis Episcoporum et Regularium, 2. ed., cura A. Bizzarri Archiepiscopi Philippensis Secretarii edita, Romae: Ex Typographia Polyglotta S. C. de Prop. Fide, 1885.

Corpus Iuris Civilis, 3 vols., Vol. III, *Novellae,* quas recognivit R. Schoell, et absolvit G. Kroll, ed. stereotypa 5., Berolini, 1928.

Decretales D. Gregorii Papae IX, una cum glossis restitutae, 2 vols., Romae, 1582.

Decretum Gratiani emendatum et notationibus illustratum una cum glossis Gregorii XIII Pont. Max. iussu editum, 2 vols., Romae, 1582.

Jaffé, Philippus, *Regesta Pontificum Romanorum ab condita Ecclesia ad annum post Christum natum MCXCVIII,* 2. ed. correctam et auctam auspiciis Gulielmi Wattenbach curaverunt F. Kaltenbrunner, P. Ewald, S. Loewenfeld, 2 vols. in 1, Lipsiae, 1885-1888.

Liber Sextus Decretalium D. Bonifatii Papae VIII, suae integritati una cum Clementinis et Extravagantibus, earumque Glossis restitutis, Romae, 1582.

Mansi, Joannes, *Sacrorum Conciliorum Nova et Amplissima Collectio,* 53 vols. in 60, Parisiis, Arnhem, Lipsiae, 1901-1927.

Monumenta Germaniae Historica, Legum Sectio II, Capitularia Regum Francorum, 2 tomes, Tom. I, ed. Alfredus Boretius, Hannoverae, 1883, Tom. II, edd. Alfredus Boretius et V. Krause, Hannoverae, 1890-1897.

———, *Legum Sectio III, Concilia,* 2 tomes, Tom. I, ed. Fridericus Maassen, Hannoverae, 1893; Tom. II, ed. Albertus Werminghoff, Hannoverae, 1904-1908.

Potthast, Augustus, *Regesta Pontificum Romanorum inde ab anno post Christum natum MCXCVIII ad annum MCCCIV,* 2 vols., Berolini, 1874-1875.

Von der Hardt, Hermann, *Magnum et Oecumenicum Constantiense Concilium,* 6 vols. in 3, Francofurti et Lipsiae, 1697-1700.

Reference Works

Abbo, John—Hannan, Jerome, *The Sacred Canons,* 2 vols., St. Louis: B. Herder Book Co., 1952.

Acta Congressus Iuridici Internationalis, 5 vols., Romae: Libraria Pont. Instituti Utriusque Iuris, 1935-1937.

Annuari Pontificio per l'anno 1952, Città del Vaticano: Tipografia Poliglotta Vaticana, 1952.

Augustine, Charles, *A Commentary on the New Code of Canon Law,* 8 vols., Vol. III, 2. ed., St. Louis: B. Herder Co., 1919.

Bachofen, Augustinus, *Compendium Juris Regularium,* Neo Eboraci, 1903.

Bail, M. Ludovicus, *Summa Conciliorum Omnium,* rev. ed., 2 vols., Patavii, 1723.

Berutti, Christophorus, *Institutiones Iuris Canonici,* 6 vols. in 7, Vol. III, Taurini-Romae: Marietti, 1936.

Beste, Udalricus, *Introductio in Codicem,* 3 ed., Collegeville, Minn.: St John's Abbey Press, 1946.

Bouscaren, T. Lincoln—Ellis, Adam, *Canon Law,* 2 rev. ed., Milwaukee: The Bruce Publishing Co., 1951.

Bouix, D., *Tractatus de Iure Regularium,* 2 vols., Parisiis, 1857.

Cappello, Felix, *Summa Iuris Canonici,* 3 vols., Vol. II, 4. ed., Romae: Apud Aedes Universitatis Gregorianae, 1945.

Chelodi, Ioannes, *Ius Canonicum de Personis,* 3. ed. curavit Pius Ciprotti, Vincenza: Società Anonima Tipografica, 1942.

Clancy, Patrick, *Secular Institutes,* Washington, D. C.: The Canon Law Society of America, 1952.

Cocchi, Guidus, *Commentarium in Codicem Iuris Canonici ad usum scholarum,* 8 vols., Vol. IV (Liber II, *De Personis,* Pars II, *De Religiosis*), 4. ed., Taurinorum Augustae: Ex Officina Libraria Marietti, 1946.

Comyns, Joseph, *Papal and Episcopal Administration of Church Property,* The Catholic University of America Canon Law Studies, n. 147, Washington, D. C.: The Catholic University of America Press, 1942.

Cook, John, *Ecclesiastical Communities and Their Ability to Induce Legal Customs,* The Catholic University of America Canon Law Studies, n. 300, Washington, D. C.: The Catholic University of America Press, 1950.

Coronata, Matthaeus Conte a, *Institutiones Iuris Canonici ad Usum Utriusque Cleri et Scholarum,* 5 vols., Vol| 1, 2. ed., Taurini: Marietti, 1939.

Crescentius a Cartosio, P., *De Virginibus in Primaeva Ecclesia Latina Earumque Juridicis Obligationibus ad Perfectionem,* Romae: Pontificia Universitas Gregoriana, 1943.

Creusen, Josephus, *De Juridica Status Religiosi Evolutione,* 2. ed., Romae: Apud Aedes Pontificae Universitatis Gregorianae, 1948.

———, *Religious Men and Women in the Code,* translated by E. F. Garesché, 4. English ed. by A. C. Ellis, Milwaukee: The Bruce Publishing Co., 1940.

Currier, Charles, *History of Religious Orders,* New York, 1894.

De Carlo, Camillus, *Jus Religiosorum,* Tornaci: Desclée et Socii, 1950.

De Institutis Saecularibus, 1 vol., incomplete, cura et studio *Commentarium pro Religiosis,* Romae, 1951.

Fanfani, Ludovicus, *De Iure Religiosorum,* 3. ed., Rovigo: Istituto Padano di Arti Grafiche, 1949.

Farell, Benjamin, *The Rights and Duties of the Local Ordinary Regarding Congregations of Women Religious of Pontifical Approval,* The Catholic University of America Canon Law Studies, n. 128, Washington, D. C.: The Catholic University of America Press, 1941.

Field, Charlotte, *Guidance and Vocational Choice with Special Reference to the Single Life,* Typewritten Masters Dissertation: The Catholic University of America, Washington, D. C., 1951.

Fogliasso, Aemilius, *Introductio in vigentem disciplinam de iuridicis relationibus inter religiones et ordinarium loci,* Augustae Taurinorum: Schola Typographica Salesiana, 1948.

Freriks, Celestine, *Religious Congregations in Their External Relations,* The Catholic University of America Canon Law Studies, n. 1, Washington, D. C.: The Catholic University of America, 1916.

Frey, Wolfgang, *The Act of Religious Profession,* The Catholic University of America Canon Law Studies, n. 63, Washington, D. C.: The Catholic University of America, 1931.

Gallik, George, *The Rights and Duties of Bishops Regarding Diocesan Sisterhoods,* St. Paul, Minn.: Wanderer Publishing Co., 1939.

Hannan, Jerome, *The Canon Law of Wills,* The Catholic University of America Canon Law Studies, n. 86, Washington, D. C.: The Catholic University of America, 1934.

Hefele, Carolus—Leclercq, Henricus, *Histoire des Conciles,* 11 vols. in 21, Paris: Letouzey et Ané, 1901-1952.

Heimbucher, Max, *Die Orden und Kongregationen der katholischen Kirche,* 3. ed., 2 vols., Paderborn: Ferdinand Schöningh, 1933-1934.

Helyot, Pierre, *Histoire des ordres monastiques, religieux et militaires, et des congrégations séculières,* 8 vols., Parisiis, 1714-1719.

Heston, Edward, *The Alienation of Church Property in the United States,* The Catholic University of America Canon Law Studies, n. 132, Washington, D. C.: The Catholic University of America Press, 1941.

Hostiensis, Cardinalis (Henricus de Segusio), *Commentaria in Quinque Decretalium Libros,* 5 vols. in 3, Venetiis, 1581.

Jone, Heribert, *Commentarium in Codicem Iuris Canonici,* 2 vols., incomplete, Paderborn: Officina Libraria F. Schöningh, 1950-1952.

Kettlewell, Samuel, *Thomas à Kempis and the Brothers of the Common Life,* 2. ed., abridged, London, 1885.

Konrad, Joseph, *The Transfer of Religious to Another Community,* The Catholic University of America Canon Law Studies, n. 278, Washington, D. C.: The Catholic University of America Press, 1949.

Kurtscheid, Bertrandus, *Historia Iuris Canonici, Historia Institutorum,* Vol. I, *Ab Ecclesiae Fundatione usque ad Gratianum,* Romae: Officium Libri Catholici, 1941.

Lynch, Timothy, *Contracts between Bishops and Religious Congregations,* The Catholic University of America Canon Law Studies, n. 239, Washington, D. C.: The Catholic University of America Press, 1946.

McFarland, Norman, *Religious Vocation—Its Juridic Concept,* Typewritten Licentiate Dissertation: The Catholic University of America, Washington, D. C., 1950.

McManus, James, *The Administration of Temporal Goods in Religious Institutes,* The Catholic University of America Canon Law Studies, n. 109, Washington, D. C.: The Catholic University of America, 1937.

Michiels, Gommarus, *Normae Generales Juris Canonici,* 2. ed., 2 vols., Parisiis—Tornaci—Romae: Desclée et Socii, 1949.

Migne, Jacques Paul, *Patrologiae Cursus Completus, Series Graeca,* 161 vols. in 164, Parisiis, 1857-1866.

———, *Patrologiae Cursus Completus, Series Latina,* 221 vols., Parisiis, 1844-1864.

Moeder, John, *The Proper Bishop for Ordination and Dimissorial Letters,* The Catholic University of America Canon Law Studies, n. 95, Washington, D. C.: The Catholic University of America, 1935.

Molitor, Raphael, *Religiosi Iuris Capita Selecta,* Ratisbonae, 1909.

Montalembert, Charles, *The Monks of the West,* 7 vols., authorized translation, Edinburgh and London: William Blackwood and Sons, 1861-1879.

Muzzarelli, Vincentius, *De Professione Religiosa a Primordiis ad Saec. XII,* Romae: Apud Piam Societatem Sancti Pauli, 1938.

———, *Tractatus Canonicus de Congregationibus Iuris Diocesani,* Romae: Apud Piam Societatem a S. Paulo Apostolo, 1943.

O'Neill, Francis, *The Dismissal of Religious in Temporary Vows,* The Catholic University of America Canon Law Studies, n. 166, Washington, D. C.: The Catholic University of America Press, 1942.

Orth, Clement, *The Approbation of Religious Institutes,* The Catholic University of America Canon Law Studies, n. 71, Washington, D. C.: The Catholic University of America, 1931.

Parsons, Anscar, *Canonical Elections,* The Catholic University of America Canon Law Studies, n. 118, Washington, D. C.: The Catholic University of America Press, 1939.

Pejška, Joseph, *Jus Canonicum Religiosorum,* 3. ed., Friburgi Brisgoviae: Herder, 1927.

Piatus Montensis (Jean Joseph Loiseaux), *Praelectiones Juris Regularis,* 2. ed., 2 vols., Tornaci, 1896.

Proceedings of the Conference on Secular Institutes, ed. Joseph E. Haley, Chicago: Fides Publishers, 1952.

Quinn, Stephen, *Relation of the Local Ordinary to Religious of Diocesan Approval,* The Catholic University of America Canon Law Studies, n. 283, Washington, D. C.: The Catholic University of America Press, 1949.

Regatillo, Eduardus, *Interpretatio et Iurisprudentia Codicis Iuris Canonici,* Santander, Sal Terrae, 1949.

Reilly, Thomas, *The Visitation of Religious,* The Catholic University of America Canon Law Studies, n. 112, Washington, D. C.: The Catholic University of America, 1938.

Reinmann, Gerald, *The Third Order of St. Francis,* The Catholic University of America Canon Law Studies, n. 50, Washington, D. C.: The Catholic University of America, 1928.

Ristuccia, Bernard, *Quasi-Religious Societies,* The Catholic University of America Canon Law Studies, n. 261, Washington, D. C.: The Catholic University of America Press, 1949.

Rothoff, *Le Droit des Sociétés sans Voeux,* Bruges: Desclée de Brouwer, 1949.

Schaefer, Timotheus, *De Religiosis ad Normam Iuris Canonici,* 4. ed., Romae: Typis Polyglottis Vaticanis, 1947.

Schmalzgrueber, Franciscus, *Ius Ecclesiasticum Universum,* 5 vols. in 12, Romae, 1843-1845.

Schroeder, H. J., *Disciplinary Decrees of the General Councils,* St. Louis: B. Herder Book Co., 1937.

Secular Institutes, London: Blackfriars Publications, 1952.

Sipos, Stephanus, *Enchiridion Iuris Canonici,* Pécs: Ex Typographia "Haladàs R. T.," 1926.

Sister M. Hildegarda, *The Apostolic Movement of Schoenstatt and the Schoenstatt Sisters of Mary of the Catholic Apostolate,* Cape Town, South Africa: The Standard Press, 1949.

Sister M. Monica, *Angela Merici and Her Teaching Ideal,* New York: Longmans, Green, and Co., 1927.

Society of the Daughters of the Heart of Mary, no author, publisher, or date given.

Stanton, William, *De Societatibus sive Virorum sive Mulierum in Communi Viventium sine Votis,* 2. ed., Halifaxiae: Apud custodiam librariam maioris seminarii a Sanctissimo Corde B. M. V., 1936.

Suarez, Franciscus, *Opera Omnia,* 26 vols. in 28, editio nova a Carolo Berton, Parisiis: Apud Ludovicum Vivès, 1856-1868.

Thomas Aquinas, S., *The Religious State,* ed. John Proctor, Westminster: The Newman Press, 1950.

———, *Summa Theologica,* 22. ed., 6 vols., Taurini-Romae: Marietti, 1939.

Van Hove, Alphonsus, *Commentarium Lovaniense in Codicem Iuris Canonici,* Vol. I, Tom. 1, *Prolegomena ad Codicem Iuris Canonici,* 2. ed., Mechliniae-Romae: H. Dessain, 1945.

Vermeersch, Arthurus—Creusen, Josephus, *Epitome Iuris Canonici,* 3 vols., Vol. I, 7. ed., Mechlinae-Romae: H. Dessain, 1949.

Waters, Joseph, *The Probation in Societies of Quasi-Religious,* The Catholic University of America Canon Law Studies, n. 306, Washington, D. C.: The Catholic University of America Press, 1951.

Wernz, Franciscus—Vidal, Petrus, *Ius Canonicum ad Codicis Normam Textus Iuris Canonici,* 6 vols., Romae, 1898-1914.

Wernd, Franciscus—Vidal, Petrus, *Ius Canonicum ad Codicis Normam Exactum,* 7 tomes in 8 vols., Tom. III, *De Religiosis,* Romae: Apud Aedes Universitatis Gregorianae, 1933.

Woywod, Stanislaus, *A Practical Commentary on the Code of Canon Law,* revised by Callistus Smith, revised and enlarged edition, 2 vols., New York: Joseph F. Wagner, Inc., 1948.

Articles

"Adnotationes," *ME,* LXXV (1950), 171-183.

B., M.-T., "Une Réalisation Contemporaine: L'Institution thérèsienne," *La Vie Spirituelle,* LXXI (July-December, 1949), 108-112.

———, "A Teresian Institute," *Life of the Spirit,* IV (1949-1950), 563-566.

Benedict, Leola, "New Wine in New Bottles," *St. Anthony Messenger,* Vol. LVIII, No. 10 (March, 1951), pp. 4-6.

Bergh, "Les Instituts Séculiers," *NRT,* LXX (1948), 1052-1062.

Boland, E., "The Grail Movement," *The Month,* Vol. CLXII, No. 829 (July, 1933), pp. 42-51.

Canals, Salvador, "De Institutis Saecularibus," *ME,* LXXIV (1949), 151-164.

———, "Los Institutos Seculares de Perfeccion y Apostolado," *Revista Española de Derecho Canonico,* II (1947), 821-861.

Carpentier, René, "Constitution Apostolique 'Provida Mater Ecclesia,'" *NRT,* LXIX (1947), 417-430.

Conway, W., "Important New Decree on *Negotiatio," IER,* 5. series, LXXIV (1950), 366-371.

———, "Important New Law for 'Secular Institutes,'" *IER,* 5. series, LXIX (1947), 1011-1014.

Creusen, Josephus, 'Commercè Interdit," *RCR,* XXII (1950), 184-191.

———, "Formes Modernes de Vie Religieuse," *RCR,* VIII (1932), 1-15.

———, "Instituts Séculiers," *RCR,* XXI (1949), 124; XXII (1950), 28-30.

———, "Les Instituts Séculiers," *RCR,* XX (1948), 133-141, 165-178.

———, "Sociétés religieuses," *ETL,* XI (1934), 778-186.

Delchard, A., "Commentaire," *NRT,* LXXII (1950), 732-737.

———, "Etat de perfection, voeux et consécration dans les instituts séculiers," *RDC,* I (1951), 281-299.

Deman, T., "Le groupe des Filles de Sainte Catherine de Sienne," *La Vie Spirituelle,* LXXVIII (January-June, 1948), 471-476.

———, "The Daughters of St. Catherine of Siena," (translation by Mary Barbour), *The Torch,* Vol. XXXII, No. 9 (November, 1948), pp. 23-26.

Farina, Leonard, "Miss Morris Makes a Movie," *The Lamp,* Vol. XLIX, No. 5 (May, 1951), pp. 20-22, and 30.

Gambari, Aelius, "Institutorum Saecularium et Congregationum Religiosarum evolutio comparata," *De Institutis Saecularibus,* I, 311-368.

Goyeneche, Servus, "Annotationes ad Const. Ap. 'Provida Mater Ecclesia'," *Apollinaris,* XX (1947), 15-37.

———, "De votis simplicibus in fontibus et in doctrina in ordine ad statum religiosum constituendum," *Acta Congressus Iuridici Internationalis,* IV, 301-315.

Guay, André, "Les Instituts séculiers," *RUO,* XVIII (1948), 5*-21*, 77*-103*.

Gutiérrez, Anastasius, "De gradibus libertatis et subiectionis religiosorum respectu ordinarii loci," *CpRM,* XXII (1941), 28-37, 83-92, 133-143, 213-227, 305-313; XXIII (1942), 30-41, 113-124, 292-298.

———, "De vetita clericis et religiosis negotiatione seu mercatura," *CpRM,* XXIX (1950), 183-211; XXX (1951), 151-159.

———, "Doctrina generalis theologica et iuridica de statu perfectionis evangelicae et comparatio inter eiusdem diversos gradus ab Ecclesia iuridice ordinatos," *De Institutis Saecularibus,* I, 252-310.

Heston, Edward, "The Government of Secular Institutes," *Secular Institutes,* pp. 89-104.

"Holy See Approves Lay Religious Group," *The Monitor,* Vol. XCII, No. 28 (September 16, 1949), p. 7.

"Instituts Séculiers," *Analecta Juris Pontificii,* XVII (1888), 424-446, 689-710; XVIII (1889), 800-827.

Jombart, Emile, "Un état de perfection au milieu du monde," *RDC,* II (1952), 57-77.

———, "Un Nouvel Etat de Perfection, Les Instituts Séculiers," *RAM,* XXIV (1948), 269-281.

L., A.—G., A., "Iurisprudentiae pro Institutis saecularibus hucusque condita summa lineamenta," *De Institutis Saecularibus,* I, 198-234.

LaPuma, Vincenzo, "Evoluzione del Diritto dei Religiosi da Pio IX a Pio XI," *Acta Congressus Iuridici Internationalis,* IV, 193-203.

Larraona, Arcadius, "Commentarium Codicis," *CpR,* I (1920), 16-21, 45-50, 133-140, 171-177, 209-217, 345-349; II (1921), 134-139, 168-172, 201-210, 275-287; V (1924), 41-49.

———, "Constitutionis 'Provida Mater Ecclesia,' pars altera," *De Institutis Saecularibus,* I, 23-148.

———, "De secreto a Superioribus ecclesiasticis circa Instituta servando," *De Institutis Saecularibus,* I, 188-190.

Lauwers, C., "Societates sine votis et status canonicus perfectionis," *ETL,* XXVIII (1952), 59-89, 215-238.

Lemoine, Robert, "Commentary on the Constitution 'Provida Mater'," *Secular Institutes,* pp. 66-88.

"Les Oblats de St. Benoît," *Revue Bénédictine,* III (1886-1887, 55-61, 107-111, 156-160, 209-220, 249-255.

Maroto, Philippus, "Annotationes," *CpR,* IX (1928), 294-296.

———, "Consultationes," *CpR,* V (1924), 242-252.

McReavy, Lawrence, "Negotiatio Clericis Prohibita," *The Clergy Review,* XXVI (July-December, 1951), 1-13.

O'Connor, John, "The Covenant of Love," *The Missionary Servánt,* Vol. XXIV, No. 3 (March, 1951), pp. 5-9.

———, "Secular Institutes: a new apostolate," *America,* LXXXIV (October, 1949-April, 1950), 223-225.

Onclin, W., "Chronica Actorum Sanctae Sedis," *ETL,* XXIV (1948), 456-462.

Peinador, Antonius, "De perfectione Christiana," *CpRM,* XXIX (1950), 44-60.

Plus, Raoul, "Une fondation hollandaise: les dames de Nazareth," *La Vie Spirituelle,* LXXVIII (January-June, 1948), 463-470.

Pond, K., "A Carmelite Lay Institute," *Life of the Spirit,* IV (1949-1950), 125-129.

Sister M. Monica, "The Democratic Company of St. Angela," *Catholic World,* CLXXI (1950), 178-184.

Smiddy, Thomas, "Negotiatio," *The Jurist,* XI (1951), 486-519.

Steiger, A. P., "De propagatione et diffusione vitae religiosae," *Periodica,* XIII (1924), 29-60, 73-100, 153-180.

Sullivan, J. P., "Lay Communities," *The Commonweal,* LI (October, 1949-April, 1950), 344.

Thorman, Donald, "Opus Dei," *St. Anthony Messenger,* Vol. LVIII, No. 3(August, 1950), pp. 17-19, and 23.

"Traité des congrégations séculières," *Analecta Juris Pontificii,* V (1861), 52-103, 147-217.

"Twentieth Century Nuns Wear Jewelry, Colored Dresses," *The Monitor,* Vol. XCIV, No. 47 (February 8, 1952), p. 3.

Vermeersch, Arthurus, "De status religiosi essentia et interpretatione can. 487 et 488," *Periodica,* XV (1926), 1-13.

Periodicals

America, New York, 1909—

Analecta Juris Pontificii, Romae, 1855-1869; Parisiis, 1872-1891.

Apollinaris, Romae, 1928—

Catholic World, The, New York, 1865—

Clergy Review, The, London, 1931—

Commentarium pro Religiosis, Romae, 1920-1934; ab anno 1935; *Commentarium pro Religiosis et Missionariis.*

Commonweal, The, New York, 1924—

Ephemerides Theologicae Lovanienses, Lovanii, 1924—

Irish Ecclesiastical Record, The, Dublin, 1864—

Jurist, The, Washington, D. C., 1941—

Lamp, The, New York, 1903—

Life of the Spirit, Oxford, 1947—

Missionary Servant, The, New York, 1928—

Monitor, The, San Francisco, 1858—

Monitore Ecclesiastico, Il, Romae: 1876-1948; ab anno 1949: *Monitor Ecclesiasticus.*

Month, The, London, 1864—

Nouvelle Revue Théologique, Paris, 1869—

Osservatore Romano, L', Roma, 1861-1929; Città del Vaticano, 1929—

Periodica de Religiosis et Missionariis, Brugis, 1905-1919; ab anno 1920: *Periodica de Re Canonica et Morali utilia praesertim Religiosis et Missionariis,* Brugis, 1920-1927; ab anno 1927: *Periodica de Re Morali, Canonica, Liturgica,* Brugis, 1927-1936, et Romae, 1937—

Revista Española de Derecho Canonico, Salamanca, 1946—

Revue Bénédictine, Bruges, 1884—

Revue d'Ascétique et de Mystique, Toulouse, 1910—

Revue de Droit Canonique, Strasbourg, 1951—

Revue de l'Université d'Ottawa, Ottawa, 1930—

Revue des Communautés Religieuses, Louvain, 1925—

St. Anthony Messenger, Cincinnati, 1893—

Torch, The, New York, 1916—

Vie Spirituelle, La, Paris, 1919—

Abbreviations

AAS—*Acta Apostolicae Sedis.*

ASS—*Acta Sanctae Sedis.*

Bruns—*Canones Apostolorum et Conciliorum Saeculorum IV-VIII.*

Bull. Rom. Taur.—*Bullarium Romanum, Tauriensis Editio.*

Bull. Rom. Cont.—*Bullarii Romani Continuatio Summorum Pontificum.*

c.—canon seu caput (iuris antiqui).

can.—canon (novi Codicis).

Conc. Trident.—Concilium Tridentium.

CpR(M)—*Commentarium pro Religiosis* (*et Missionariis*).

ETL—*Ephemerides Theologicae Lovanienses.*

Fontes—*Codicis Iuris Canonici Fontes,* cura... Gasparri editi.

IER—*The Irish Ecclesiastical Record.*

JE—Jaffé, Philippus, *Regesta Pontificum Romanorum* (edited by P. Ewald; for the years 590-882).

JK—Jaffé, *op. cit.* (edited by F. Kaltenbrunner; to the year 590).

JL—Jaffé, *op. cit.* (edited by S. Loewenfeld; for the years 882-1198).

Mansi—*Sacrorum Conciliorum Nova et Amplissima Collectio.*

ME—*Il Monitore Ecclesiastico* (*Monitor Ecclesiasticus*).

MGH—*Monumenta Germaniae Historica.*

MPG—(Migne, *Patrologia Graeca*), Migne, Jacques Paul, *Patrologiae Cursus Completus, Series Graeca.*

MPL—(Migne, *Patrologia Latina*), Migne, Jacques Paul, *Patrologiae Cursus Completus, Series Latina.*

NRT—*Nouvelle Revue Théologique.*

Periodica—*Periodica de Religiosis et Missionariis,* etc.

Potthast—*Regesta Pontificum Romanorum inde ab anno post Christum natum MCXCVIII ad annum MCCCIV.*

RAM—*Revue d'Ascétique et de Mystique.*

RCR—Revue des Communautés Religieuses.
RDC—Revue de Droit Canonique.
RUO—Revue de l'Université d'Ottawa.
S. C. de Prop. Fide—Sacra Congregatio de Propaganda Fide.
S. C. Ep. et Reg.—Sacra Congregatio Episcoporum et Regularium.
S. C. super Statu Regularium—Sacra Congregatio super Statu Regularium.
S. C. de Religiosis—Sacra Congregatio de Religiosis.
s.v.—sub verbo; sub verbis.

ALPHABETICAL INDEX

Abbot *nullius,* 99
Angela Merici, St., 44
Antony, St., 10
Apostolate, dedication to, 62-63, 85
Apostolic administrator, 99
Approval, papal, 64, 106-108
Associations of the faithful and secular Institutes, 64, 67-69, 77, 83, 84-85, 100, 104, 113
Athanasius, St., 11
Augustine, St., 14

Basil the Great, St., 11
Bishops,
  right of foundation, 98-101
  special faculties of, 104
  cf. Ordinary, local
Beghards, 23-24
Beguines, 23-24
Benedict, St., 11-12
Brothers of the Common Life, 25-27, 37
Bruno, St., 12

Canons and Canonesses, 14-16
Charles Borromeo, St., 38
Chastity, obligation of, 88
Chrodegang of Metz, 14
Columban, St., 11
Common houses, 94-97
Common life,
  in formal sense, 72-73, 93
  in material sense, 72-73, 95
Congregation of the Council, 82-83
Congregation for the Propagation of the Faith, 81-83
Congregation of Religious, 78-82, 99-101, 107-108, 115, 121
Councils
  Aix-la-Chapelle, 14, 15
  Ancyra, 79
  Beziers, 24
  Chalcedon, 9, 12, 13
  Chalon-sur-Saon, 15
  Cologne, 24
  Eichstatt, 24
  Elvira, 7, 9
  Fritzlar, 24
  Lateran, IV General Council of, 18, 19, 21
  Lyons, II General Council of, 19
  Mainz, 24
  Orleans III, 9
  Rome, 8
  Toledo I, 9
  Trent, 28
  Trier, 24
  Valence, 9
  Vienne, 24
Cyprian, St., 7

Decree of erection, 104
Decree of praise, 106-109
Dominic, St., 20

English Ladies, The, 29-30
Eusebius, St., 14
Exemption of secular Institutes, 112

Felix of Valois, St., 17
Frances of Rome, St., 27
Francis de Sales, St., 44
Francis of Assisi, 20-22

Gerson, John, 26
Grabow, Matthew, 26
Gratian, 9-10

Holy See,
  permission to found Institutes, 98-101
  quinquennial report to, 75
  requirements for approval by, 105-108
Holzhauser, Ven., 38

Incorporation into secular Institutes, 92-94

Jesuits, simple vows of, 33-34
John Eudes, St., 38
John Gualbert, St., 12

Marcella, St., 11
Martin of Tours, St., 11
Mendicant Orders, 20-21

Military Orders, 16-18
Monasticism, 10-13

Negotiatio, 90-92

Obedience, obligation of, 89
Oblates of St. Frances of Rome, 27
Olier, Father, 38
Ordinary, local
  rights of, 111-112
  cf. also bishops

Pachomius, St., 11
Patrick, St., 11
Paul the Hermit, St., 10
Peter Nolasco, St., 17
Philip Neri, St., 37
Popes
  Benedict XIII, 29
  Benedict XIV, 29
  Boniface VIII, 16, 19
  Callistus II, 17
  Clement V, 17
  Clement IX, 29
  Clement XII, 29
  Eugene IV, 27
  Gregory XIII, 34, 37
  Honorius III, 20
  Innocent I, 9
  Innocent III, 17, 21
  John XXII, 24
  Leo the Great, 9
  Leo XIII, 31, 36, 46, 47, 48, 51
  Nicholas IV, 22
  Paul V, 37
  Pius V, St., 28, 33
  Pius IX, 35, 46
  Pius XI, 53, 56
  Pius XII, 51
  Urban II, 16
Prefect apostolic, 99, 100

Quasi-Religious Societies
  cf. Societies of the Common Life
Quinquennial report to Holy See, 75

Raymond of Pennafort, St., 17-18
Robert, St., 12
Romuald, St., 12

Secular Institutes
  Constitutions of, 78-79, 87, 88-90, 92, 95, 103, 106, 107
  distinct from Associations of the faithful, 64, 67-69, 79, 83, 113
  distinct from religious institutes, 70-74, 103, 120
  distinct from Societies of the Common Life, 70, 74, 120
  distinct from Third Orders Secular, 62, 83, 113
  divisions of, 63-64, 109
  essential elements of, 84-97
  establishment of, 97-109
  exemption of, 112
  government of, 112-117
  independence of, 116-117
  law for, 67-69, 76-79
  members in wide sense, 86-87
  moral personality of, 65, 77, 92, 99
  name of, 64-67
  nature of, 61-62, 65-66, 117
  not bound by law for religious, 70, 74-76, 87, 89
  prior to 1947, 47-51, 118-121
  purpose of, 62-63
  subjection to local ordinary, 110-112
Societies of the Common Life, 16, 36-41, 73, 90, 106
  designation of, 41-43
State of perfection
  juridic, 5-6
  notion of, 4
  secular Institutes, 80-81
  Societies of the Common Life, 40-41

Terminology used in secular Institutes, 117
Third Orders Secular
  distinct from secular Institutes, 62, 83, 113
  history of, 22-23
Thomas Aquinas, St., 4

Vicar apostolic, 99, 100
Vicar capitular, 99
Vicar general, 99
Vincent de Paul, St., 38, 44
Virgins in early church, 6-7
Vows
  in secular Institutes, 74, 85-92, 120
  private, 38-39, 71-72
  public, in secular Institutes, 120
  semi-public, 72
  simple, permitted, 29-32, 34, 36
  social, 72
  solemn, required for religious state, 19, 28, 32, 33, 35, 36

BIOGRAPHICAL NOTE

DONNELL ANTHONY WALSH was born on June 15, 1922, in Oakland, California. He received his elementary education at Sacred Heart and Our Lady of Lourdes Schools in that city. In September, 1935, he entered St. Joseph's College, Mountain View, Calif., the preparatory seminary of the Archdiocese of San Francisco. On graduation from St. Joseph's College in 1941 he entered St. Patrick's Seminary, Menlo Park, Calif., where he received the degree of Bachelor Arts in June, 1943. He was ordained to the priesthood at St. Mary's Cathedral, San Francisco, on June 15, 1946. After four years as Assistant Pastor of St. Brigid's Church, San Francisco, he was assigned to the Catholic University of America to pursue a course of studies in Canon Law. He received the de gree of Bachelor of Canon Law in June, 1951, and the degree of Licentiate in Canon Law in June, 1952.

CANON LAW STUDIES *

337. Bourque, Rev. John R., S.T.L., J.C.L., The Judicial Power of the Church—Canon 1553, § 1.
338 .Cornell, Rev. Charles E., A.B., S.T.B., J.C.L., The Juridical Status of Heretics and Schismatics in Good Faith.
339. Fitzgerald, Rev. William Francis, A.B., S.T.L., J.C.L., The Parish Census and the *Liber Status Animarum*.
340. Kubik, Rev. Stanislaus J., S.T.D., J.C.L., Invalidity of Dispensations according to canon 84, § 1.
341. Nugent, Rev. John Gerard, C.M., J.C.L., Ordination in Societies of the Common Life.
342. Peterson, Rev. Casimir Melvyn, *S.S., A.B., S.T.L., J.C.L.,* Spiritual Care in Diocesan Seminaries.
343. Reiss, Rev. John Charles, A.B., S.T.L., J.C.L., The Time and Place of Sacred Ordination.
344. Sheehan, Rev. Joseph George, J.C.L., The Obligation of Respect and Obedience of Clerics to their Ordinary—Canon 127.
345. Shekleton, Rev. Matthew M., O.S.M., J.C.L., Doctrinal Interpretation of Law.
346. Viau, Rev. Roger, S.T.L., J.C.L., Doubt in Canon Law.
347. Walsh, Rev. Donnell Anthony, A.B., J.C.L., The New Law on Secular Institutes.

---

* For a complete list of the available numbers of this series apply to the Catholic University of America Press, 620 Michigan Avenue, N.E., Washington 17, D.C.

www.ingramcontent.com/pod-product-compliance
Lightning Source LLC
LaVergne TN
LVHW050219080826
844660LV00012B/439

* 9 7 8 0 8 1 3 2 2 5 1 5 9 *